Adonais : 1821

Shelley, Percy Bysshe

Contents

ADONAIS : 1821

BY

Shelley, Percy Bysshe

PREFACE

Adonais is the first writing by Shelly which has been included in the Claren-don Press Series. It is a poem of convenient length for such a purpose, being neither short nor decidedly long; and—leaving out of count some of the short poems—is the single one by this author which approaches to being 'popular.' It is elevated in sentiment, classical in form,—in substance, biographical in relation to Keats, and in some minor degree autobiographical for Shelly himself. On these grounds it claimed a reasonable preference over all his other poems, for the present method of treatment; although some students of Shelly, myself included, might be disposed to maintain that, in point of absolute intrinsic beauty and achievement, and of the qualities most especially characteristic of its author, it is not superior, or indeed is but barely equal, to some of his other compositions. To take, for instance, two poems not very different in length from Adonais—The Witch of Atlas *is more original, and* Epipsychindion more abstract in ideal.

I have endeavoured to present in my introductory matter a comprehensive account of all particulars relevant to *Adonais* itself, and to Keats as its subject, and Shelly as its author. The accounts here give of both these great poets are of course meager, but I assume them to be not insufficient for our immediate and restricted purpose. There are many other books which the reader can profitably consult as to the life and works of Shelley; and three or four (at least) as to the life and works of Keats. My concluding notes are, I suppose, ample in scale: if they are excessive, that is an involuntary error on my part. My aim in them has been to illustrate and elucidate the poem in its details, yet without travelling far afield in search of remote analogies or discursive comment—my wish being rather to 'stick to my text': wher-ever a difficulty presents itself, I have essayed to define it, and clear it up—but not always to my own satisfaction. I have seldom had to discuss the opinions of previous writers on the same points, for the simple reason that of detailed criticism of **Adonais**, apart from merely textual memoranda, there is next to none.

It has appeared to me to be part of my duty to point out here and there, but by no means frequently, some special beauty in the poem; occasionally also something which seems to me defective or faulty. I am aware that this latter is an invidious office, which naturally exposes one to an imputation, from some quarters, of obtuseness, and, from others, of presumption; none the less I have expressed myself with the frankness which, according to my own view, belongs to the essence of such a task as is here undertaken. **Adonais** is a composition which has retorted beforehand upon its actual or possible detractors. In the poem itself, and in the prefatory matter adjoined to it, Shelley takes critics very severely to task: but criticism has its discerning and temperate, as well as its 'stupid and malignant,' phases.

W. M. ROSSETTI.
July 1890.

MEMOIR OF SHELLEY

THE life of Percy Bysshe Shelley is one which has given rise to a great deal of controversy, and which cannot, for a long time to come, fail to be regarded with very diverse sentiments. His extreme opinions on questions of religion and morals, and the great latitude which he allowed himself in acting according to his own opinions, however widely they might depart from the law of the land and of society, could not but produce this result. In his own time he was generally accounted an outrageous and shameful offender. At the present date many persons entertain essentially the same view, although softened by lapse of years, and by respect for his standing as a poet: others regard him as a conspicuous reformer. Some take a medium course, and consider him to have been sincere, and so far laudable; but rash and reckless of consequences, and so far censurable. His poetry also has been subject to very different constructions. During his lifetime it obtained little notice save for purposes of disparagement and denunciation. Now it is viewed with extreme enthusiasm by many, and is generally admitted to hold a permanent rank in English literature, though faulty (as some opine) through vague idealism and want of backbone. These are all points on which I shall here offer no personal opinion. I shall confine myself to tracing the chief outlines of Shelley's life, and (very briefly) the sequence of his literary work.

Percy Bysshe Shelley came of a junior and comparatively undistinguished branch of a very old and noted family. His branch was termed the Worminghurst Shelleys; and it is only quite lately [Footnote 1: See the **Life of Mrs. Shelley,** by Lucy Madox Rossetti (**Eminent Women Series**), published in 1890. The connexion between the two branches of the Shelley family is also set forth—incidentally, but with perfect distinctness—in Collins's **Peerage of England** (1756), vol. iii. p. 119. He says that Viscount Lumley (who died at some date towards 1670) 'married Frances, daughter of Henry Shelley, of Warminghurst in Sussex, Esq. (a younger branch of the family seated at Michaelgrove, the seat of the present Sir John Shelley, Bart.).'] that the affiliation of this branch to the more eminent and senior stock of the Michelgrove Shelleys has passed from the condition of a probable and obvious surmise into that of an established fact. The family traces up to Sir William Shelley, Judge of the Common Pleas under Henry VII, thence to a Member of Parliament in 1415, and to the reign of Edward I, or even to the Norman Conquest. The Worminghurst Shelleys start with Henry Shelley, who died in 1623. It will be sufficient here to begin with the poet's grandfather, Bysshe Shelley. He was born at Christ Church, Newark, North America, and raised to a noticeable height, chiefly by two wealthy marriages, the fortunes of the junior branch. Handsome, keen-minded, and adventurous, he eloped with Mary Catherine, heiress of the Rev. Theobald Michell, of Horsham; after her death he eloped with Elizabeth Jane, heiress of Mr. Perry, of Penshurst. By this second wife he had a family, now represented by the Baron de l'Isle and Dudley: by his first wife he had (besides a daughter) a son Timothy, who was the poet's father, and who became in due course Sir Timothy Shelley, Bart., M.P. His baronetcy was inherited from his father Bysshe—on whom it had been conferred in 1806, chiefly through the interest of the Duke of Norfolk, the head of the Whig party in the county of Sussex, to whose politics the new baronet had adhered.

Mr. Timothy Shelley was a very ordinary country gentleman in essentials, and a rather eccentric one in some details. He was settled at Field Place, near Horsham, Sussex, and married Elizabeth, daughter of Charles Pilfold, of Effingham, Surrey; she was a beauty, and a woman of good abilities, but without any literary turn. Their first child was the poet, Percy Bysshe, born at Field Place on Aug. 4, 1792: four daughters also grew up, and a younger son, John: the eldest son of John was afterwards the Baronet, having succeeded, in 1889, Sir Percy Florence Shelley, the poet's only surviving son. No one has managed to discover in the parents of Percy Bysshe any qualities furnishing the prototype or the nucleus of his poetical genius, or of the very exceptional cast of mind and character which he developed in other directions. The parents were commonplace: if we go back to the grandfather, Sir Bysshe, we encounter a man who was certainly not commonplace, but who seems to have been devoid of any fervour of spirit, whether in the poetical or in any other direction. He figures as intent upon his worldly interests, accumulating a massive fortune, and spending lavishly upon the building of Castle Goring; in his old age, penurious, unsocial, and almost churlish in his habits. His passion was to domineer and carry his point; of this the poet may have inherited something. His ideal of success was wealth and worldly position, things to which the poet was, on the contrary, abnormally indifferent.

Shelley's schooling began at six years of age, when he was placed under the Rev. Mr. Edwards, at Warnham. At ten he went to Sion House School, Brentford, of which the Principal was Dr. Greenlaw, the pupils being mostly sons of local tradesmen. In July, 1804, he proceeded to Eton, where Dr. Goodall was the Head Master, succeeded, just towards the end of Shelley's stay, by the far severer Dr. Keate. Shelley was shy, sensitive, and of susceptible fancy: at Eton we first find him insubordinate as well. He steadily resisted the fagging-system, learned more as he chose than as his masters dictated, and was known as 'Mad Shelley,' and 'Shelley the Atheist.' It has sometimes been said that an Eton boy, if rebellious, was termed 'Atheist,' and that the designation, as applied to Shelley, meant no more than that. I do not feel satisfied that this is true at all; at any rate it seems to me probable that

Shelley, who constantly called himself an atheist in after-life, received the epithet at Eton for some cause more apposite than disaffection to school-authority.

He finally left Eton in July, 1810. He had already been entered at University College, Oxford, in April of that year, and he commenced residence there in October. His one very intimate friend in Oxford was Thomas Jefferson Hogg, a student from the county of Durham. Hogg was not, like Shelley, an enthusiast eager to learn new truths, and to apply them; but he was a youth appreciative of classical and other literature, and little or not at all less disposed than Percy to disregard all prescription in religious dogma. By demeanour and act they both courted academic censure, and they got it in its extremest form. Shelley wrote, probably with some co-operation from Hogg, and he published anonymously in Oxford, a little pamphlet called *The Necessity of Atheism;* he projected sending it round broadcast as an invitation or challenge to discussion. This small pamphlet—it is scarcely more than a flysheet—hardly amounts to saying that Atheism is irrefragably true, and Theism therefore false; but it propounds that the existence of a God cannot be proved by reason, nor yet by testimony; that a direct revelation made to an individual would alone be adequate ground for convincing that individual; and that the persons to whom such a revelation is not accorded are in consequence warranted in remaining unconvinced. The College authorities got wind of the pamphlet, and found reason for regarding Shelley as its author, and on March 25, 1811, they summoned him to appear. He was required to say whether he had written it or not. To this demand he refused an answer, and was then expelled by a written sentence, ready drawn up. With Hogg the like process was repeated. Their offence, as entered on the College records, was that of 'contumaciously refusing to answer questions,' and 'repeatedly declining to disavow' the authorship of the work. In strictness therefore they were expelled, not for being proclaimed atheists, but for defying academic authority, which required to be satisfied as to that question. Shortly before this disaster an engagement between Shelley and his first cousin on the mother's side, Miss Harriet Grove, had come to an end, owing to the alarm excited by the youth's sceptical opinions.

Settling in lodgings in London, and parting from Hogg, who went to York to study conveyancing, Percy pretty soon found a substitute for Harriet Grove in Harriet Westbrook, a girl of fifteen, schoolfellow of two of his sisters at Clapham. She was exceedingly pretty, daughter of a retired hotel-keeper in easy circumstances. Shelley wanted to talk both her and his sisters out of Christianity; and he cultivated the acquaintance of herself and of her much less juvenile sister Eliza, calling from time to time at their father's house in Chapel Street, Grosvenor Square. Harriet fell in love with him: besides, he was a highly eligible *parti,* being a prospective baronet, absolute heir to a very considerable estate, and contingent heir (if he had assented to a proposal of entail, to which however he never did assent, professing conscientious objections) to another estate still larger. Shelley was not in love with Harriet; but he liked her, and was willing to do anything he could to further her wishes and plans. Mr. Timothy Shelley, after a while, pardoned his son's misadventure at Oxford, and made him a moderate allowance of £200 a-year. Percy then visited a cousin in Wales, a member of the Grove family. He was recalled to London by Harriet Westbrook, who protested against a project of sending her back to school. He counselled resistance. She replied in July 1811 (to quote a contemporary letter from Shelley to Hogg), 'that resistance was useless, but that she would fly with me, and threw herself upon my protection.' This was clearly a rather decided step upon the damsel's part: we may form our own conclusions whether she was willing to unite with Percy without the bond of marriage; or whether she confidently calculated upon inducing him to marry her, her family being kept in the dark; or whether the whole affair was a family manœuvre for forcing on an engagement and a wedding. Shelley returned to London, and had various colloquies with Harriet: in due course he eloped with her to Edinburgh, and there on August 28 he married her. His age was then just nineteen, and hers sixteen. Shelley, who was a profound believer in William Godwin's *Political Justice,* rejected the institution of marriage as being fundamentally irrational and wrongful. But he saw that he could not in this instance apply his own pet theories without involving in discredit and discomfort the woman whose love had been bestowed upon him. Either his opinion or her happiness must be sacrificed to what he deemed a prejudice of society: he decided rather to sacrifice the former.

For two years, or up to an advanced date in 1813, the married life of Shelley and Harriet appears to have been a happy one, so far as their mutual relation was concerned; though rambling and scrambling, restricted by mediocrity of income (£400 a year, made up between the two fathers), and pestered by the continual, and to Percy at last very offensive, presence of Miss Westbrook as an inmate of the house. They lived in York, Keswick in Cumberland, Dublin (which Shelley visited as an express advocate of Catholic emancipation and repeal of the Union), Nantgwillt in Radnorshire, Lynmouth in Devonshire, Tanyrallt in Carnarvonshire, London, Bracknell in Berkshire: Ireland and Edinburgh were also revisited. Various strange adventures befell; the oddest of all being an alleged attempt at assassination at Tanyrallt. Shelley asserted it, others disbelieved it: after much disputation the biographer supposes that, if not an imposture, it was a romance, and, if not a romance, at least a hallucination,—Shelley, besides being wild in talk and wild in fancy, being by this time much addicted to laudanum-dosing. In June 1813 Harriet gave birth, in London, to her first child, Ianthe Eliza (she married a Mr. Esdaile, and died in 1876). About the same time Shelley brought out his earliest work of importance, the poem of **Queen Mab:** its speculative audacities were too extreme for publication, so it was only privately printed.

Amiable and accommodating at first, and neither ill-educated nor stupid, Harriet did not improve in tone as she advanced in womanhood. Her sympathy or tolerance for her husband's ideals and vagaries flagged; when they differed she gave him the cold shoulder; she wanted luxuries—such as a carriage of her own—which he neither cared for nor could properly afford. He even said—and one can hardly accuse him of saying it insincerely—that she had been unfaithful to him: this however remains quite unproved, and may have been a delusion. He sought the society of the philosopher Godwin, then settled as a bookseller in Skinner Street, Holborn. Godwin's household at this time consisted of his second wife, who had been a Mrs. Clairmont; Mary, his daughter by his first wife, the celebrated Mary Wollstonecraft; and his young son by his second wife, William; also his step-children, Charles and Clare Clairmont, and Fanny Wollstonecraft (or Imlay), the daughter of Mary Wollstonecraft by her first irregular union with Gilbert Imlay. Until May 1814, when she was getting on towards the age of seventeen, Shelley had scarcely set eyes on Mary Godwin: he then saw her, and a sudden passion sprang up between them—uncontrollable, or, at any rate, uncontrolled. Harriet Shelley has left it on record that the advances and importunities came from Mary Godwin to Shelley, and were for a while resisted: it was natural for Harriet to allege this, but I should not suppose it to be true, unless in a very partial sense. Shelley sent for his wife, who had gone for a while to Bath (perhaps in a fit of pettishness, but this is not clear), and explained to her in June that they must separate—a resolve which she combated as far as seemed possible, but finally she returned to Bath, staying there with her father and sister. Shelley made some arrangements for her convenience, and on July 28 he once more eloped, this time with Mary Godwin. Clare Clairmont chose to accompany them. Godwin was totally opposed to the whole transaction, and Mrs. Godwin even pursued the fugitives across the Channel; but her appeal was unavailing, and the youthful and defiant trio proceeded in much elation of spirit, and not without a good deal of discomfort at times, from Calais to Paris, and thence to Brunen by the Lake of Uri in Switzerland. It is a curious fact, and shows how differently Shelley regarded these matters from most people, that he wrote to Harriet in affectionate terms, urging her to join them there or reside hard by them. Mary, before the elopement took place, had made a somewhat similar proposal. Harriet had no notion of complying; and, as it turned out, the adventurers had no sooner reached Brunen than they found their money exhausted, and they travelled back in all haste to London in September,—Clare continuing to house with them now, and for the most part during the remainder of Shelley's life. Even a poet and idealist might have been expected to show a little more worldly wisdom than this. After his grievous experiences with Eliza Westbrook, the sister of his first wife, Shelley might have managed to steer clear of Clare Clairmont, the sister by affinity of his second partner in life. He would not take warning, and he paid the forfeit: not indeed that Clare was wanting in fine qualities both of mind and of character, but she proved a constant source of excitement and uneasiness in the household, of unfounded scandal, and of harassing complications.

In London Shelley and Mary lived in great straits, abandoned by almost all their acquaintances, and playing hide-and-seek with creditors. But in January 1815 Sir Bysshe Shelley died, and Percy's money affairs improved greatly. An arrangement was arrived at with his father, whereby he received a regular annual income of

£1000, out of which he assigned to Harriet £200 for herself and her two children—a son, Charles Bysshe, having been born in November 1814 (he died in 1826). Shelley and Mary next settled at Bishopgate, near Windsor Forest. In May 1816 they went abroad, along with Miss Clairmont and their infant son William, and joined Lord Byron on the shore of the Lake of Geneva. An amour was already going on between Byron and Miss Clairmont; it resulted in the birth of a daughter, Allegra, in January 1817: she died in 1822, very shortly before Shelley. He and Mary had returned to London in September 1816. Very shortly afterwards, November 9, the ill-starred Harriet Shelley drowned herself in the Serpentine: her body was only recovered on December 10, and the verdict of the Coroner's jury was 'found drowned,' her name being given as 'Harriet Smith.' The career of Harriet since her separation from her husband is very indistinctly known. It has indeed been asserted in positive terms that she formed more than one connexion with other men: she had ceased to live along with her father and sister, and is said to have been expelled from their house. In these statements I see nothing either unveracious or unlikely: but it is true that a sceptical habit of mind, which insists upon express evidence and upon severe sifting of evidence, may remain unconvinced [Footnote 1: I am indebted to Mr. J. Cordy Jeaffreson for some strongly reasoned arguments, in private correspondence, tending to Harriet's disculpation.]. This was the second suicide in Shelley's immediate circle, for Fanny Wollstonecraft had taken poison just before under rather unaccountable circumstances. No doubt he felt dismay and horror, and self-reproach as well; yet there is nothing to show that he condemned his conduct, at any stage of the transactions with Harriet, as heinously wrong. He took the earliest opportunity—December 30—of marrying Mary Godwin; and thus he became reconciled to her father and to other members of the family.

It was towards the time of Harriet's suicide that Shelley, staying in and near London, became personally intimate with the essayist and poet, Leigh Hunt, and through him he came to know John Keats: their first meeting appears to have occurred on February 5, 1817. As this matter bears directly upon our immediate theme, the poem of *Adonais,* I deal with it at far greater length than its actual importance in the life of Shelley would otherwise warrant.

Hunt, in his ***Autobiography,*** narrates as follows: 'I had not known the young poet [Keats] long when Shelley and he became acquainted under my roof. Keats did not take to Shelley as kindly as Shelley did to him. Shelley's only thoughts of his new acquaintance were such as regarded his bad health with which he sympathised [this about bad health seems properly to apply to a date later than the opening period when the two poets came together], and his poetry, of which he has left such a monument of his admiration as ***Adonais.*** Keats, being a little too sensitive on the score of his origin, felt inclined to see in every man of birth a sort of natural enemy. Their styles in writing also were very different; and Keats, notwithstanding his unbounded sympathies with ordinary flesh and blood, and even the transcendental cosmopolitics of ***Hyperion,*** was so far inferior in universality to his great acquaintance that he could not accompany him in his daedal rounds with Nature, and his Archimedean endeavours to move the globe with his own hands [an allusion to the motto appended to ***Queen Mab***]. I am bound to state thus much; because, hopeless of recovering his health, under circumstances that made the feeling extremely bitter, an irritable morbidity appears even to have driven his suspicions to excess; and this not only with regard to the acquaintance whom he might reasonably suppose to have had some advantages over him, but to myself, who had none; for I learned the other day with extreme pain . . . that Keats, at one period of his intercourse with us, suspected both Shelley and myself of a wish to see him undervalued! Such are the tricks which constant infelicity can play with the most noble natures. For Shelley let ***Adonais*** answer.' It is to be observed that Hunt is here rather putting the cart before the horse. Keats (as we shall see immediately) suspected Shelley and Hunt 'of a wish to see him undervalued' as early as February 1818; but his 'irritable morbidity' when 'hopeless of recovering his health' belongs to a later date, say the spring and summer of 1820.

It is said that in the spring of 1817 Shelley and Keats agreed that each of them would undertake an epic, to be written in a space of six months: Shelley produced ***The Revolt of Islam*** (originally entitled ***Laon and Cythna***), and Keats produced ***Endymion.*** Shelley's poem, the longer of the two, was completed by the early autumn, while Keats's occupied him until the winter which opened 1818. On October 8, 1817, Keats wrote to a friend, 'I refused to visit Shelley, that I might have my own unfettered scope'; meaning presumably that he wished to finish *Endymion* according to his own canons of taste and execution, without being hampered by any advice from Shelley. There is also a letter from Keats to his two brothers, December 22, 1817, saying: 'Shelley's poem [*Laon and Cythna*] is out, and there are words about its being objected to as much as *Queen Mab* was. Poor Shelley, I think he has his quota of good qualities.' As late as February 1818 he wrote, 'I have not yet read Shelley's poem.' On January 23 of the same year he had written: 'The fact is, he [Hunt] and Shelley are hurt, and perhaps justly, at my not having showed them the affair [*Endymion* in MS.] officiously; and, from several hints I have had, they appear much disposed to dissect and anatomize any trip or slip I may have made.' It was at nearly the same date, February 4, that Keats, Shelley, and Hunt wrote each a sonnet on *The Nile:* in my judgement, Shelley's is the least successful of the three.

Soon after their marriage, Shelley and his second wife settled at Great Marlow, in Buckinghamshire. They were shortly disturbed by a Chancery suit, whereby Mr. Westbrook sought to deprive Shelley of the custody of his two children by Harriet, Ianthe and Charles. Towards March 1818, Lord Chancellor Eldon pronounced judgement against Shelley, on the ground of his culpable conduct as a husband, carrying out culpable opinions upheld in his writings. The children were handed over to Dr. Hume, an army-physician named by Shelley: he had to assign for their support a sum of £120 per annum, increased to £200 by a supplement from Mr. Westbrook. About the same date he suffered from an illness which he regarded as a dangerous pulmonary attack, and he made up his mind to quit England for Italy; accompanied by his wife, their two infants William and Clara, Miss Clairmont, and her infant Allegra, who was soon afterwards consigned to Lord Byron in Venice. Mr. Charles Cowden Clarke, who was Keats's friend from boyhood, writes: 'When Shelley left England for Italy, Keats told me that he had received from him an invitation to become his guest, and in short to make one of his household. It was upon the purest principle that Keats declined his noble proffer, for he entertained an exalted opinion of Shelley's genius—in itself an inducement. He also knew of his deeds of bounty, and from their frequent social intercourse he had full faith in the sincerity of his proposal. . . . Keats said that, in declining the invitation, his sole motive was the consciousness, which would be ever prevalent with him, of his being, in its utter extent, not a free agent, even within such a circle as Shelley's—he himself nevertheless being the most unrestricted of beings.' Mr. Clarke seems to mean in this passage that Shelley, ***before*** starting for Italy, invited Keats to accompany him thither—a fact, if such it is, of which I find no trace elsewhere. It is however just possible that Clarke was only referring to the earlier invitation, previously mentioned, for Keats to visit at Great Marlow; or he may most probably, with some confusion as to dates and details, be thinking of the message which Shelley, when already settled in Italy for a couple of years, addressed to his brother-poet—of which more anon.

Shelley and his family—including for the most part Miss Clairmont—wandered about a good deal in Italy. They were in Milan, Leghorn, the Bagni di Lucca, Venice and its neighbourhood, Rome, Naples, Florence, Pisa, the Bagni di Pisa, and finally (after Shelley had gone to Ravenna by himself) in a lonely house named Casa Magni, between Lerici and San Terenzio, on the Bay of Spezzia. Their two children died; but in 1819 another was born, the Sir Percy Florence Shelley who lived on till November 1889. They were often isolated or even solitary. Among their interesting acquaintances at one place or another were, besides Byron, Mr. and Mrs. Gisborne (the latter had previously been Mrs. Reveley, and had been sought in marriage by Godwin after the death of Mary Wollstonecraft in 1797); the Contessina Emilia Viviani, celebrated in Shelley's poem of ***Epipsychidion;*** Captain Medwin, Shelley's cousin and schoolfellow; the Greek Prince, Alexander Mavrocordato; Lieutenant and Mrs. Williams, who joined them at Casa Magni; and Edward John Trelawny, an adventurous and daring sea-rover, who afterwards accompanied Byron to Greece.

It was only towards the summer of 1819 that Shelley read the ***Endymion.*** He wrote of it thus in a letter to his publisher, Mr. Ollier, September 6, 1819: 'I have read . . . Keats's poem. . . . Much praise is due to me for having read it, the author's intention appearing to be that no person should possibly get to the end of it. Yet it is full of some of the highest and the finest gleams of poetry: indeed, everything seems to be viewed by the mind of a poet which is described in it. I think, if he had printed about fifty pages of fragments from it, I should have been led to admire Keats as a poet more than I ought—of which there is now no danger.' Shelley regarded the

Hymn to Pan, in the first Book of **Endymion,** as affording 'the surest promise of ultimate excellence.'

The health of Keats having broken down, and consumption having set in, Shelley wrote to him from Pisa urging him to come over to Italy as his guest. Keats did not however go to Pisa, but, along with the young painter Joseph Severn, to Naples, and thence to Rome. I here subjoin Shelley's letter.

'Pisa—July 27, 1820.
'MY DEAR KEATS,

'I hear with great pain the dangerous accident you have undergone [recurrence of blood-spitting from the lungs], and Mr. Gisborne, who gives me the account of it, adds that you continue to wear a consumptive appearance. This consumption is a disease particularly fond of people who write such good verses as you have done, and, with the assistance of an English winter, it can often indulge its selection. I do not think that young and amiable poets are bound to gratify its taste: they have entered into no bond with the Muses to that effect. But seriously (for I am joking on what I am very anxious about) I think you would do well to pass the winter in Italy, and avoid so tremendous an accident; and, if you think it as necessary as I do, so long as you continue to find Pisa or its neighbourhood agreeable to you, Mrs. Shelley unites with myself in urging the request that you would take up your residence with us. You might come by sea to Leghorn (France is not worth seeing, and the sea is particularly good for weak lungs)—which is within a few miles of us. You ought, at all events, to see Italy; and your health, which I suggest as a motive, may be an excuse to you. I spare declamation about the statues and paintings and ruins, and (what is a greater piece of forbearance) about the mountains and streams, the fields, the colours of the sky, and the sky itself.

'I have lately read your **Endymion** again, and even with a new sense of the treasures of poetry it contains—though treasures poured forth with indistinct profusion. This people in general will not endure; and that is the cause of the comparatively few copies which have been sold. I feel persuaded that you are capable of the greatest things, so you but will. I always tell Ollier to send you copies of my books. ***Prometheus Unbound*** I imagine you will receive nearly at the same time with this letter. Italic: ***The Cenci*** I hope you have already received: it was studiously composed in a different style.

"Below the good how far! but far above the ***great*** [Footnote 1: This line (should be '***Beneath*** the good,' &c.) is the final line of Gray's ***Progress of Poesy.*** The sense in which Shelley intends to apply it to ***The Cenci*** may admit of some doubt. He seems to mean that ***The Cenci*** is not equal to really good tragedies; but still is superior to some tragedies which have recently appeared, and which bad critics have dubbed great.]!" In poetry I have sought to avoid system and mannerism. I wish those who excel me in genius would pursue the same plan.

'Whether you remain in England, or journey to Italy, believe that you carry with you my anxious wishes for your health and success—wherever you are, or whatever you undertake—and that I am

'Yours sincerely,
'P. B. SHELLEY.'

Keats's reply to Shelley ran as follows:—

'Hampstead—August 10, 1820.

'MY DEAR SHELLEY,

'I am very much gratified that you, in a foreign country, and with a mind almost over-occupied, should write to me in the strain of the letter beside me. If I do not take advantage of your invitation, it will be prevented by a circumstance I have very much at heart to prophesy. [Footnote 1: This phrase is not very clear to me. From the context ensuing, it might seem that the 'circumstance' which prevented Keats from staying with Shelley in Pisa was that his nerves were in so irritable a state as to prompt him to move from place to place in Italy rather than fix in any particular city or house.]. There is no doubt that an English winter would put an end to me, and do so in a lingering hateful manner. Therefore I must either voyage or journey to Italy, as a soldier marches up to a battery. My nerves at present are the worst part of me: yet they feel soothed that, come what extreme may, I shall not be destined to remain in one spot long enough to take a hatred of any four particular bedposts.

'I am glad you take any pleasure in my poor poem—which I would willingly take the trouble to unwrite if possible, did I care so much as I have done about reputation.

'I received a copy of *The Cenci,* as from yourself, from Hunt. There is only one part of it I am judge of—the poetry and dramatic effect, which by many spirits nowadays is considered the Mammon. A modern work, it is said, must have a purpose, which may be the God. An artist must serve Mammon: he must have "self-concentration"—selfishness perhaps. You, I am sure, will forgive me for sincerely remarking that you might curb your magnanimity, and be more of an artist, and load every rift of your subject with ore. The thought of such discipline must fall like cold chains upon you, who perhaps never sat with your wings furled for six months together. And is not this extraordinary talk for the writer of *Endymion,* whose mind was like a pack of scattered cards? I am picked up and sorted to a pip. My imagination is a monastery, and I am its monk.

'I am in expectation of *Prometheus* every day. Could I have my own wish effected, you would have it still in manuscript, or be but now putting an end to the second Act. I remember you advising me not to publish my first blights, on Hampstead Heath [Footnote 1: Though Shelley gave this advice, which was anything but unsound, he is said to have taken good-naturedly some steps with a view to getting the volume printed. Mr. John Dix, writing in 1846, says: 'He [Shelley] went to Charles Richards, the printer in St. Martin's Lane, when quite young, about the printing a little volume of Keats's first poems.']. I am returning advice upon your hands. Most of the poems in the volume I send you [this was the volume containing *Lamia, Hyperion,* &c.] have been written above two years [Footnote 2: This statement is not correct—so far at least as the longer poems in the volume are concerned. *Isabella* indeed was finished by April, 1818; but *Hyperion* was not relinquished till late in 1819, and *The Eve of St. Agnes* and *Lamia* were probably not even begun till 1819.], and would never have been published but for hope of gain: so you see I am inclined enough to take your advice now.

'I must express once more my deep sense of your kindness, adding my sincere thanks and respects for Mrs. Shelley. In the hope of soon seeing you I remain

'Most sincerely yours,
'JOHN KEATS.'

It may have been in the interval between writing his note of invitation to Keats, and receiving the reply of the latter, that Shelley penned the following letter to the Editor of the *Quarterly Review* —the periodical which had taken (or had shared with *Blackwood's Magazine*) the lead in depreciating *Endymion.* The letter, however, was left uncompleted, and was not dispatched. (I omit such passages as are not directly concerned with Keats.)

'SIR,

'Should you cast your eye on the signature of this letter before you read the contents, you might imagine that they related to a slanderous paper which appeared in your Review some time since. . . . I am not in the habit of permitting myself to be disturbed by what is said or written of me. . . . The case is different with the unfortunate subject of this letter, the author of *Endymion,* to whose feelings and situation I entreat you to allow me to call your attention. I write considerably in the dark; but, if it is Mr. Gifford that I am addressing, I am persuaded that, in an appeal to his humanity and justice, he will acknowledge the *fas ab hoste doceri.* I am aware that the first duty of a reviewer is towards the public; and I am willing to confess that the *Endymion* is a poem considerably defective, and that perhaps it deserved as much censure as the pages of your Review record against it. But, not to mention that there is a certain contemptuousness of phraseology, from which it is difficult for a critic to abstain, in the review of *Endymion,* I do not think that the writer has given it its due praise. Surely the poem, with all its faults, is a very remarkable production for a man of Keats's age [Footnote 1: See p. 97 as to Shelley's underrating of Keats's age. He must have supposed that Keats was only about twenty years old at the date when *Endymion* was completed. The correct age was twenty-two.]; and the promise of ultimate excellence is such as has rarely been afforded even by such as have afterwards attained high literary eminence. Look at book 2, line 833, &c., and book 3, lines 113 to 120; read down that page, and then again from line 193 [Footnote 2: The passages to which Shelley refers begin thus: 'And then the forest told it in a dream;' 'The rosy veils mantling the East;' 'Upon a weeded rock this old man sat.']. I could cite many other passages to convince you that it deserved milder usage. Why it should have been reviewed at all, excepting for the purpose of bringing its excellences into notice, I cannot conceive; for it was very little read, and there was no danger that it should become a model to the age of that false taste with which I confess that it is replenished.

'Poor Keats was thrown into a dreadful state of mind by this review, which, I am persuaded, was not written with any intention of producing the effect—to which it has at least greatly contributed—of embittering his existence, and inducing a disease from which there are now but faint hopes of his recovery. The first effects are described to me to have resembled insanity, and it was by assiduous watching that he was restrained from effecting purposes of suicide. The agony of his sufferings at length produced the rupture of a blood-vessel in the lungs, and the usual process of consumption appears to have begun. He is coming to pay me a visit in Italy; but I fear that, unless his mind can be kept tranquil, little is to be hoped from the mere influence of climate.

'But let me not extort anything from your pity. I have just seen a second volume, published by him evidently in careless despair. I have desired my bookseller to send you a copy: and allow me to solicit your especial attention to the fragment of a poem entitled *Hyperion,* the composition of which was checked by the review in question. The great proportion of this piece is surely in the very highest style of poetry. I speak impartially, for the canons of taste to which Keats has conformed in his other compositions are the very reverse of my own. I leave you to judge for yourself: it would be an insult to you to suppose that, from motives however honourable, you would lend yourself to a deception of the public.'

The question arises, How did Shelley know what he here states—that Keats was thrown, by reading the *Quarterly* article, into a state resembling insanity, that he contemplated suicide, &c.? Not any document has been published whereby this information could have been imparted to Shelley: his chief informant on the subject appears to have been Mr. Gisborne, who had now for a short while returned to England, and some confirmation may have come from Hunt. As to the statements themselves, they have, ever since the appearance in 1848 of Lord Houghton's *Life of Keats,* been regarded as very gross exaggerations: indeed, I think the tendency has since then been excessive in the reverse direction, and the vexation occasioned to Keats by hostile criticism has come to be underrated.

Shelley addressed to Keats in Naples another letter, 'anxiously enquiring about his health, offering him advice as to the adaptation of diet to the climate, and concluding with an urgent invitation to Pisa, where he could assure him every comfort and attention.' Shelley did not, however, reinvite Keats to his own house on the present occasion; writing to Miss Clairmont, 'We are not rich enough for that sort of thing.' The letter to Miss Clairmont is dated February 18, 1821, and appears to have been almost simultaneous with the one sent to Keats. In that case, Keats cannot be supposed to have received the invitation; for he had towards the middle of November quitted Naples for Rome, and by February 18 he was almost at his last gasp.

Shelley's feeling as to Keats's final volume of poems is further exhibited in the following extracts. (To Thomas Love Peacock, November, 1820.) 'Among the modern things which have reached me is a volume of poems by Keats; in other respects insignificant enough, but containing the fragment of a poem called *Hyperion.* I dare say you have not time to read it; but it is certainly an astonishing piece of writing, and gives me a conception of Keats which I confess I had not before.' (To Mrs. Leigh Hunt, November 11, 1820.) 'Keats's new volume has arrived to us, and the fragment called *Hyperion* promises for him that he is destined to become one of the first writers of the age. His other things are imperfect enough [Footnote 1: I do not find in Shelley's writings anything which distinctly modifies this opinion. However, his biographer, Captain Medwin, avers that Shelley valued all the poems in Keats's final volume: he cites especially *Isabella* and *The Eve of St. Agnes.*], and, what is worse, written in the bad sort of style which is becoming fashionable among those who fancy that they are imitating Hunt and Wordsworth. . . . Where is Keats now? I am anxiously expecting him in Italy, when I shall take care to bestow every possible attention on him. I consider his a most valuable life, and I am deeply interested in his safety. I intend to be the physician both of his body and his soul,—to keep the one warm, and to teach the other Greek and Spanish. I am aware indeed, in part, that I am nourishing a rival who will far surpass me; and this is an additional motive, and will be an added pleasure.' (To Peacock, February 15, 1821.) 'Among your anathemas of the modern attempts in poetry do you include Keats's *Hyperion* ? I think it very fine. His other poems are worth little; but, if the *Hyperion* be not grand poetry, none has been produced by our contemporaries.' There is also a phrase in a letter to Mr. Ollier, written on May 14, 1820, before the actual publication of the *Lamia* volume: 'Keats, I hope, is going to show himself a great poet; like the sun, to burst through the clouds which, though dyed in the finest colours of the air, obscured his rising.'

Keats died in Rome on February 23, 1821. Soon afterwards Shelley wrote his *Adonais.* He has left various written references to *Adonais,* and to Keats in connexion with it: these will come more appropriately when I speak of that poem itself. But I may here at once quote from the letter which Shelley addressed on June 16, 1821, to Mr. Gisborne, who had sent on to him a letter from Colonel Finch [Footnote 1: In books relating to Keats and Shelley the name of this gentleman appears repeated, without any explanation of who he was. In a MS. diary of Dr. John Polidori, Byron's travelling physician (my maternal uncle), I find the following account of Colonel Finch, whom Polidori met in Milan in 1816: 'Colonel Finch, an extremely pleasant, good-natured, well-informed, clever gentleman, spoke Italian extremely well, and was very well read in Italian literature. A ward of his gave a masquerade in London upon her coming of age. She gave to each a character in the reign of Queen Elizabeth to support, without the knowledge of each other; and received them in a saloon in proper style as Queen Elizabeth. He mentioned to me that Nelli had written a Life of Galileo, extremely fair, which, if he had money by him, he would buy, that it might be published. Finch is a great admirer of architecture in Italy. Mr. Werthern, a gentleman most peaceable and quiet I ever saw, accompanying Finch, whose only occupation [I understand this to mean the occupation of Werthern, but possibly it means of Finch] is, when he arrives at a town or other place, to set about sketching, and then colouring, so that he has perhaps the most complete collection of sketches of his tour possible. He invited me (taking me for an Italian), in case I went to England, to see him; and, hearing I was English, he pressed me much more.' The name 'Werthern' is not distinctly written: should it be 'Wertheim'?], giving a very painful account of the last days of Keats, and especially (perhaps in more than due proportion) of the violence of temper which he had exhibited. Shelley wrote thus: 'I have received the heartrending account of the closing scene of the great genius whom envy and ingratitude [Footnote 1: 'Envy' refers no doubt to hostile reviewers. 'Ingratitude' refers to a statement of Colonel Finch that Keats had 'been infamously treated by the very persons whom his generosity had rescued from want and woe.' It is not quite clear who were the persons alluded to by Finch. Keats's brother George (then in America) was presumably one: he is, however, regarded as having eventually cleared himself from the distressing imputation. I know of no one else, unless possibly the painter Haydon may be glanced at: as to him also the charge appears to be too severe and sweeping.] scourged out of the world. I do not think that, if I had seen it before, I could have composed my poem. The enthusiasm of the imagination would have overpowered the sentiment. As it is, I have finished my Elegy; and this day I send it to the press at Pisa. You shall have a copy the moment it is completed. I think it will please you. I have dipped my pen in consuming fire for his destroyers: otherwise the style is calm and solemn [Footnote 2: Shelley wrote another letter on June 16—to Miss Clairmont, then in Florence. It contains expressions to nearly the same purport. 'I have received a most melancholy account of the last illness of poor Keats; which I will neither tell you nor send you, for it would make you too low-spirited. My Elegy on him is finished. I have dipped my pen in consuming fire to chastise his destroyers: otherwise the tone of the poem is solemn and exalted. I send it to the press here, and you will soon have a copy.'].'

As I have already said, the last residence of Shelley was on the Gulf of Spezzia. He had a boat built named the Ariel (by Byron, the Don Juan), boating being his favourite recreation; and on July 1, 1822, he and Lieut. Williams, along with a single sailor-lad, started in her for Leghorn, to welcome there Leigh Hunt. The latter had come to Italy with his family, on the invitation of Byron and Shelley, to join in a periodical to be called *The Liberal.* On July 8 Shelley, with his two companions, embarked to return to Casa Magni. Towards half-past six in the evening a sudden and tremendous squall sprang up. The Ariel sank, either upset by the squall, or (as some details of evidence suggest) run down near Viareggio by an Italian fishing-boat, the crew of which had plotted to plunder her of a sum of money. The bodies were eventually washed ashore; and on August 16 the corpse of Shelley was burned on the beach under the direction of Trelawny. In the pocket of his jacket had been found two books—an Aeschylus, and the *Lamia* volume, doubled back as if it had at the last moment been thrust aside. His ashes were collected, and, with the exception of the heart which was delivered to Mrs. Shelley, were buried in Rome, in the New Protestant Cemetery. The corpse of Shelley's beloved son William had, in 1819, been interred hard by, and in 1821 that of Keats, in the Old Cemetery—a space of ground which had, by 1822, been finally closed.

The enthusiastic and ideal fervour which marks Shelley's poetry could not possibly be simulated—it was a part, the most essential part, of his character. He was remarkably single-minded, in the sense of being constantly ready to do what he professed as, in the abstract, the right thing to be done; impetuous, bold, uncompromising, lavishly generous, and inspired by a general love of humankind, and a coequal detestation of all the narrowing influences of custom and prescription. Pity, which included self-pity, was one of his dominant emotions. If we consider what are the uses, and what the abuses, of a character of this type, we shall have some notion of the excellences and the defects of Shelley. In person he was well-grown and slim; more nearly beautiful than handsome; his complexion brilliant, his dark-brown but slightly grizzling hair abundant and wavy, and his eyes deep-blue, large, and fixed. His voice was high-pitched—at times discordant, but capable of agreeable modulation; his general aspect uncommonly youthful.

The roll of Shelley's publications is a long one for a man who perished not yet thirty years of age. I append a list of the principal ones, according to date of publication, which was never very distant from that of composition. Several minor productions remain unspecified.

1810. Zastrozzi, a Romance. Puerile rubbish; and the same may be said of the next three.

1810. Original Poetry, by Victor and Cazire. Withdrawn, and for many years unknown. Published in 1898.

1810. Posthumous Fragments of Margaret Nicholson. Partly (it would appear) intended as burlesque.

1811. St. Irvyne, or The Rosicrucian, a Romance.

1813. Queen Mab.

1817. Alastor, or the Spirit of Solitude, and other Poems. The earliest volume fully worthy of its author.

1818. Laon and Cythna—reissued as The Revolt of Islam.

1819. Rosalind and Helen, a modern Eclogue, and other Poems. The character of 'Lionel' is an evident idealization of Shelley himself.

1819. The Cenci, a Tragedy.

1819. Prometheus Unbound, a Lyrical Drama, and other Poems. The Prometheus ranks as at once the greatest and the most thoroughly characteristic work of Shelley.

1819. Oedipus Tyrannus, or Swellfoot the Tyrant. A Satirical Drama on the Trial of Queen Caroline.

1821. Epipsychidion.

1821. Adonais.

1822. Hellas. A Drama on the Grecian War of Liberation.

1824. Posthumous Poems. Include Julian and Maddalo, written in 1818, The Witch of Atlas, 1820, The Triumph of Life, 1822, and many other compositions and translations.

The *Masque of Anarchy* and *Peter Bell the Third,* both written by Shelley in 1819, were published later on; also various minor poems, complete or fragmentary. *Peter Bell the Third* has a certain fortuitous connexion with Keats. It was written in consequence of Shelley's having read in the *Examiner* a notice of *Peter Bell, a Lyrical Ballad* (the production of John Hamilton Reynolds): and this notice, as has very recently been proved, was the handiwork of Keats. Shelley cannot have been aware of that fact. His prose *Essays and Letters,* including *The Defence of Poetry,* appeared in 1840. The only known work of Shelley, extant but yet unpublished, is the *Philosophical View of Reform* : an abstract of it, with several extracts, was printed in the *Fortnightly Review* in 1886.

MEMOIR OF KEATS

THE parents of John Keats were Thomas Keats, and Frances, daughter of Mr. Jennings, who kept a large livery-stable, the Swan and Hoop, in the Pavement, Moorfields, London. Thomas Keats was the principal stableman or assistant in the same business. John, a seven months' child, was born at the Swan and Hoop on October 31, 1795. Three other children grew up—George, Thomas, and Fanny. John is said to have been violent and ungovernable in early childhood. He was sent to a very well-reputed school, that of the Rev. John Clarke, at Enfield: the son Charles Cowden Clarke, whom I have previously mentioned, was an undermaster, and paid particular attention to Keats. The latter did not show any remarkable talent at school, but learned easily, and was 'a very orderly scholar,' acquiring a fair amount of Latin but no Greek. He was active, pugnacious, and popular among his school-fellows. The father died of a fall from his horse in April, 1804: the mother, after re-marrying, succumbed to consumption in February, 1810. Before the close of the same year John left school, and he was then apprenticed to a surgeon at Edmonton. In July, 1815, he passed with credit the examination at Apothecaries' Hall.

In 1812 Keats read for the first time Spenser's *Faery Queen,* and was fascinated with it to a singular degree. This and other poetic reading made him flag in his surgical profession, and finally he dropped it, and for the remainder of his life had no definite occupation save that of writing verse. From his grandparents he inherited a certain moderate sum of money—not more than sufficient to give him a tolerable start in life. He made acquaintance with Leigh Hunt, then editor of the *Examiner,* John Hunt, the publisher, Charles Wentworth Dilke, who became editor of the *Athenaeum,* the painter Haydon, and others. His first volume of *Poems* (memorable for little else than the sonnet *On Reading Chapman's Homer*) was published in 1817. It was followed by *Endymion* in April, 1818.

In June of the same year Keats set off with his chief intimate, Charles Armitage Brown (a retired Russia merchant, who afterwards wrote a book on Shakespeare's Sonnets), on a pedestrian tour in Scotland, which extended into North Ireland as well. In July, in the Isle of Mull, he got a bad sore throat, of which some symptoms had appeared also in earlier years: it may be regarded as the beginning of his fatal malady. He cut short his tour and returned to Hampstead, where he had to nurse his younger brother Tom, a consumptive invalid, who died in December of the same year.

At the house of the Dilkes, in the autumn of 1818, Keats made the acquaintance of Miss Fanny Brawne, the daughter of a gentleman independent means then dead: he was soon desperately in love with her, having 'a swooning admiration of her beauty': towards the spring of 1819 they engaged to marry, with the prospect of a long engagement. On the night of February 3, 1820, on returning to the house at Hampstead which he shared with Mr. Brown, the poet had his first attack, a violent one, of blood-spitting from the lungs. He rallied somewhat, suffered a dangerous replase in June, just prior to the publication of his final volume, containing all his best poems—*Isabella, Hyperion, The Eve of St. Agnes, Lamia,* and the leading Odes. His doctor ordered him off, as a last chance, to Italy; previously to this he had been staying in the house of Mrs. and Miss Brawne, who tended him affectionately. Keats was now exceedingly unhappy. His passionate love, his easily roused feelings of jealousy of Miss Brawne, and of suspicious rancour against even the most amicable and attached of his male intimates, the general indifference and the particular scorn and ridicule with which his poems had been received, his narrow means and uncertain outlook, and the prospect of an early death closing a painful and harassing illness—all preyed upon his mind with unrelenting tenacity. The worst of all was the sense of approaching and probably final separation from Fanny Brawne.

On September 18, 1820, he left England for Italy, in company with Mr. Joseph Severn, a student of painting in the Royal Academy, who, having won the gold medal, was entitled to spend three years abroad for advancement in his art. They travelled by sea to Naples; reached that city late in October; and towards the middle of November went on to Rome. Here Keats received the most constant and kind attention from Dr. (afterwards Sir James) Clark. But all was of no avail: after continual and severe suffering, devotedly watched by Severn, he expired on February 23, 1821. He was buried in the old Protestant Cemetery of Rome, under a little altar-tomb sculptured with a Greek lyre. His name was inscribed, along with the epitaph which he himself had composed in the bitterness of his soul, 'Here lies one whose name was writ in water.'

Keats was an undersized man, not much more than five feet high. His face was handsome, ardent, and full of expression; the hair rich, brown, and curling; the hazel eyes 'mellow and glowing—large, dark, and sensitive.' He was framed for enjoyment; but with that acuteness of feeling which turned even enjoyment into suffering, and then again extracted a luxury out of melancholy. He had vehemence and generosity, and the frankness which belongs to these qualities, not unmingled, however, with a strong dose of suspicion. Apart from the overmastering love of his closing years, his one ambition was to be a poet. His mind was little concerned either with the severe practicalities of life, or with the abstractions of religious faith.

His poems, consisting of three successive volumes, have been already referred to here. The first volume, the **Poems** of 1817, is mostly of a juvenile kind, containing only scattered suggestions of rich endowment and eventual excellence. **Endymion** is lavish and profuse, nervous and languid, the wealth of a prodigal scattered in largesse of baubles and of gems. The last volume—comprising the **Hyperion** —is the work of a noble poetic artist, powerful and brilliant both in imagination and in expression. Of the writings published since their author's death, the only one of first-rate excellence is the fragmentary **Eve of St. Mark.** There is also the drama of **Otho the Great,** written in co-operation with Armitage Brown; and in Keats's letters many admirable thoughts are admirably worded.

As to the relations between Shelley and Keats, I have to refer back to the preceding memoir of Shelley.

ADONAIS:

ITS COMPOSITION AND BIBLIOGRAPHY

FOR nearly two months after the death of Keats, February 23, 1821, Shelley appears to have remained in ignorance of the event: he knew it on or before April 19. The precise date when he began his Elegy does not seem to be recorded: one may suppose it to have been in the latter half of May. On June 5 he wrote to Mr. and Mrs. Gisborne: 'I have been engaged these last days in composing a poem on the death of Keats, which will shortly be finished; and I anticipate the pleasure of reading it to you, as some of the very few persons who will be interested in it and understand it. It is a highly wrought piece of art, and perhaps better, in point of composition, than anything I have written.'

A letter to Mr. Ollier followed immediately afterwards.

'Pisa, June 8, 1821.

'You may announce for publication a poem entitled *Adonais.* It is a lament on the death of poor Keats, with some interspersed stabs on the assassins of his peace and of his fame; and will be preceded by a criticism on *Hyperion,* asserting the due claims which that fragment gives him to the rank which I have assigned him. My poem is finished, and consists of about forty Spenser stanzas [fifty-five as published]. I shall send it to you, either printed at Pisa, or transcribed in such a manner as it shall be difficult for the reviser to leave such errors as assist the obscurity of the *Prometheus.* But in case I send it printed, it will be merely that mistakes may be avoided. I shall only have a few copies struck off in the cheapest manner. If you have interest enough in the subject, I could wish that you enquired of some of the friends and relations of Keats respecting the circumstances of his death, and could transmit me any information you may be able to collect; and especially as [to] the degree in which (as I am assured) the brutal attack in the *Quarterly Review* excited the disease by which he perished.'

The criticism which Shelley intended to write on *Hyperion* remained, to all appearance, unwritten. It will be seen, from the letter of Shelley to Mr. Severn cited further on (p. 36), that, from the notion of writing a criticism on *Hyperion* to precede *Adonais,* his intention developed into the project of writing a criticism and biography of Keats in general, to precede a volume of his entire works; but that, before the close of November, the whole scheme was given up, on the ground that it would produce no impression on an unregardful public.

In another letter to Ollier, June 11, the poet says: '*Adonais* is finished, and you will soon receive it. It is little adapted for popularity, but is perhaps the least imperfect of my compositions.'

Shelley on June 16 caused his Elegy to be printed in Pisa, 'with the types of Didot': a small quarto, and a handsome one (notwithstanding his project of cheapness); the introductory matter filling five pages, and the poem itself going on from p. 7 to p. 25. It appeared in blue paper wrappers, with a woodcut of a basket of flowers within an ornamental border. Its price was three and sixpence: of late years £40 has been given for it—probably more. Up to July 13 only one copy had reached the author's hands: this he then sent on to the Gisbornes, at Leghorn. Some copies of the Pisa edition were afterwards put into circulation in London: there was no separate English edition. The Gisbornes having acknowledged the Elegy with expressions of admiration, the poet replied as follows:

'Bagni [di Pisa], July 19.

'MY DEAREST FRIENDS,

'I am fully repaid for the painful emotions from which some verses of my poem sprung by your sympathy and approbation; which is all the reward I expect, and as much as I desire. It is not for me to judge whether, in the high praise your feelings assign me, you are right or wrong. The poet and the man are two different natures: though they exist together, they may be unconscious of each other, and incapable of deciding on each other's powers and efforts by any reflex act. The decision of the cause whether or not I am a poet is removed from the present time to the hour when our posterity shall assemble: but the court is a very severe one, and I fear that the verdict will be "Guilty—death."'

A letter to Mr. Ollier was probably a little later. It says: 'I send you a sketch for a frontispiece to the poem *Adonais.* Pray let it be put into the engraver's hands immediately, as the poem is already on its way to you, and I should wish it to be ready for its arrival. The poem is beautifully printed, and—what is of more consequence—correctly: indeed, it was to obtain this last point that I sent it to the press at Pisa. In a few days you will receive the bill of lading.' Nothing is known as to the sketch which Shelley thus sent. It cannot, I presume, have been his own production, nor yet Severn's: possibly it was supplied by Lieutenant Williams, who had some aptitude as an amateur artist.

I add some of the poet's other expressions regarding *Adonais,* which he evidently regarded with more complacency than any of his previous works—at any rate, as a piece of execution. Hitherto his favourite had been *Prometheus Unbound* : I am fain to suppose that that great effort did not now hold a second place in his affections, though he may have considered that the *Adonais,* as being a less arduous feat, came nearer to reaching its goal. (To Peacock, August, 1821.) 'I have sent you by the Gisbornes a copy of the Elegy on Keats. The subject, I know, will not please you; but the composition of the poetry, and the taste in which it is written, I do not think bad.' (To Hunt, August 26.) 'Before this you will have seen *Adonais.* Lord Byron—I suppose from modesty on account of his being mentioned in it—did not say a word of *Adonais* [Footnote 1: As Byron is introduced into *Adonais* as mourning for Keats, and as in fact he cared for Keats hardly at all, it seems possible that his silence was dictated by antagonism rather than by modesty.], though he was loud in his praise of *Prometheus,* and (what you will not agree with him in) censure of *The Cenci.* ' (To Horace Smith, September 14.) "I am glad you like *Adonais,* and particularly that you do not think it metaphysical, which I was afraid it was. I was resolved to pay some tribute of sympathy to the unhonoured dead; but I wrote, as usual, with a total ignorance of the effect that I should produce.' (To Ollier, September 25.) 'The *Adonais,* in spite of its mysticism, is the least imperfect of my compositions; and, as the image of my regret and honour for poor Keats, I wish it to be so. I shall write to you probably by next post on the subject of that poem; and should have sent the promised criticism for the second edition, had I not mislaid, and in vain sought for, the volume that contains *Hyperion.* ' (To Ollier, November 14.) 'I am especially curious to hear the fate of *Adonais.* I confess I should be surprised if *that* poem were born to an immortality of oblivion.' (To Ollier, January 11, 1822.) 'I was also more than commonly interested in the success of *Adonais.* I do not mean the sale, but the effect produced; and I should have [been] glad to have received some communication from you respecting it. I do not know even whether it has been published, and still less whether it has been republished with the alterations I sent.' As to the alterations sent nothing definite is known, but some details bearing on this point will be found in our Notes, p. 108, &c. (To Gisborne, April 10.) 'I know what to think of *Adonais,* but what to think of those who confound it with the many bad poems of the day I know not.' This expression seems to indicate that Mr. Gisborne had sent Shelley some of the current criticisms—there were probably but few in all—upon *Adonais* : to this matter I shall recur further on. (To Gisborne, June 18.) 'The *Adonais* I wished to have had a fair chance, both because it is a favourite with me, and on account of the memory of Keats—who was a poet of great genius, let the classic party say what it will.'

Earlier than the latest of these extracts Shelley had sent to Mr. Severn a copy of *Adonais,* along with a letter which I append.

'Pisa, Nov. 29th, 1821.

'DEAR SIR,

'I send you the Elegy on poor Keats, and I wish it were better worth your acceptance. You will see, by the preface, that it was written before I could obtain any particular account of his last moments. All that I still know was communicated to me by a friend who had derived his information from Colonel Finch. I have ventured [in the Preface] to express as I felt the respect and admiration which *your* conduct towards him demands.

'In spite of his transcendent genius, Keats never was, nor ever will be, a popular poet; and the total neglect and obscurity in which the astonishing remains of his mind still lie was hardly to be dissipated by a writer who, however he may differ from Keats in more important qualities, at least resembles him in that accidental one, a want of popularity.

'I have little hope therefore that the poem I send you will excite any attention, nor do I feel assured that a critical notice of his writings would find a single reader. But for these considerations, it had been my intention to have collected the remnants of his compositions, and to have published them with a Life and criticism. Has he left any poems or writings of whatsoever kind, and in whose possession are they? Perhaps you would oblige me by information on this point.

'Many thanks for the picture you promise me [presumably a portrait of Keats, but Shelley does not seem ever to have received one from Severn]: I shall consider it among the most sacred relics of the past. For my part, I little expected, when I last saw Keats at my friend Leigh Hunt's, that I should survive him.

'Should you ever pass through Pisa, I hope to have the pleasure of seeing you, and of cultivating an acquaintance into something pleasant, begun under such melancholy auspices.

'Accept, my dear Sir, the assurance of my highest esteem, and believe me

'Your most sincere and faithful servant,
'PERCY B. SHELLEY.

'Do you know Leigh Hunt? I expect him and his family here every day.'

It may have been observed that Shelley, whenever he speaks of critical depreciation of Keats, refers only to one periodical, the *Quarterly Review* : probably he did not distinctly know of any other: but the fact is that *Blackwood's Magazine* was worse than the *Quarterly.* The latter was sneering and supercilious: *Blackwood* was vulgarly taunting and insulting, and seems to have provoked Keats the more of the two, though perhaps he considered the attack in the *Quarterly* to be more detrimental to his literary standing. The *Quarterly* notice is of so much import in the life and death of Keats, and in the genesis of *Adonais,* that I shall give it, practically *in extenso,* before closing this section of my work: with *Blackwood* I can deal at once. A series of articles *On the Cockney School of Poetry* began in this magazine in October 1817, being directed mainly and very venomously against Leigh Hunt. No. 4 of the series appeared in August 1818, falling foul of Keats. It is difficult to say whether the priority in abusing Keats should of right be assigned to **Blackwood** or to the **Quarterly** : the critique in the latter review belongs to the number for April 1818, but this number was not actually issued until September. The writer of the **Blackwood** papers signed himself Z. Z. is affirmed to have been Lockhart, the son-in-law of Sir Walter Scott, and afterwards editor of the **Quarterly Review** : more especially the article upon Keats is attributed to Lockhart. A different account, as to the series in general, is that the author was John Wilson (Christopher North), revised by Mr. William Blackwood. But Z. resisted more than one vigorous challenge to unmask, and some doubt as to his identity may still remain. Here are some specimens of the amenity with which Keats was treated in **Blackwood's Magazine** :—

'His friends, we understand, destined him to the career of medicine, and he was bound apprentice some years ago to a worthy apothecary in town. . . . The frenzy of the **Poems** [Keats's first volume, 1817] was bad enough in its way; but it did not alarm us half so seriously as the calm, settled, imperturbable, drivelling idiocy of **Endymion**. . . . We hope however that, in so young a person and with a constitution originally so good, even now the disease is not utterly incurable. . . . Mr. Hunt is a small poet, but a clever man; Mr. Keats is a still smaller poet, and he is only a boy of pretty abilities which he has done everything in his power to spoil. . . . It is a better and wiser thing to be a starved apothecary than a starved poet: so back to the shop, Mr. John, back to "plaster, pills, and ointment-boxes," &c. But for Heaven's sake, young Sangrado, be a little more sparing of extenuatives and soporifics in your practice than you have been in your poetry.'

Even the death of Keats, in 1821, did not abate the rancour of **Blackwoods Magazine.** Witness the following extracts. (1823) 'Keats had been dished—utterly demolished and dished—by **Blackwood** long before Mr. Gifford's scribes mentioned his name. . . . But let us hear no more of Johnny Keats. It is really too disgusting to have him and his poems recalled in this manner after all the world thought they had got rid of the concern.' (1824) 'Mr. Shelley died, it seems, with a volume of Mr. Keats's poetry "grasped with one hand in his bosom"—rather an awkward posture, as you will be convinced if you try it. But what a rash man Shelley was to put to sea in a frail boat with Jack's poetry on board! . . . Down went the boat with a "swirl"! I lay a wager that it righted soon after ejecting Jack.' . . . (1826) 'Keats was a Cockney, and Cockneys claimed him for their own. Never was there a young man so encrusted with conceit.'

If this is the tone adopted by *Blackwood's Magazine* in relation to Keats living and dead, one need not be surprised to find that the verdict of the same review upon the poem of *Adonais,* then newly published, ran to the following effect:—

'Locke says the most resolute liar cannot lie more than once in every three sentences. Folly is more engrossing; for we could prove from the present Elegy that it is possible to write two sentences of pure nonsense out of three. A more faithful calculation would bring us to ninety-nine out of every hundred; or—as the present consists of only fifty-five stanzas—leaving about five readable lines in the entire. . . . A Mr. Keats, who had left a decent calling for the melancholy trade of Cockney poetry, has lately died of a consumption, after having written two or three little books of verses much neglected by the public. . . . The New School, however, will have it that he was slaughtered by a criticism of the *Quarterly Review* : "O flesh, how art thou fishified!" There is even an aggravation in this cruelty of the Review—for it had taken three or four years to slay its victim, the deadly blow having been inflicted at least as long since. [This is not correct: the *Quarterly* critique, having appeared in September 1818, preceded the death of Keats by two years and five months.] . . . The fact is, the *Quarterly,* finding before it a work at once silly and presumptuous, full of the servile *slang* that Cockaigne dictates to its servitors, and the vulgar indecorums which that Grub Street Empire rejoiceth to applaud, told the truth of the volume, and recommended a change of manners [Footnote 1: *Blackwood* seems to imply that the *Quarterly* accused *Endymion* of indecency: this is not correct.] and of masters to the scribbler. Keats wrote on; but he wrote *indecently,* probably in the indulgence of his social propensities.'

The virulence with which Shelley, as author of *Adonais,* was assailed by *Blackwood's Magazine,* is the more remarkable, and the more symptomatic of partisanship against Keats and any of his upholders, as this review had in previous instances been exceptionally civil to Shelley, though of course with some serious offsets. The notices of *Alastor, Rosalind and Helen,* and *Prometheus Unbound* —more especially the first—in the years 1819 and 1820, would be found to bear out this statement.

From the dates already cited, it may be assumed that the Pisan edition of *Adonais* was in London in the hands of Mr. Ollier towards the middle of August 1821, purchasable by whoever might be minded to buy it. Very soon afterwards it was reprinted in the *Literary Chronicle and Weekly Review,* published by Limbird in the Strand—December 1, 1821: a rather singular, not to say piratical, proceeding. An editorial note was worded thus: 'Through the kindness of a friend, we have been favoured with the latest production of a gentleman of no ordinary genius, Mr. Bysshe Shelley. It is an elegy on the death of a youthful poet of considerable promise, Mr. Keats, and was printed at Pisa. As the copy now before us is perhaps [surely not] the only one that has reached England, and the subject is one that will excite much interest, we shall print the whole of it.' This promise was not literally fulfilled, for stanzas 19 to 24 were omitted, not apparently with any special object.

After the publication in London of the Pisan edition of *Adonais,* the poem remained unreprinted until 1829. It was then issued at Cambridge, at the instance of Lord Houghton (Mr. Richard Monckton Milnes) and Mr. Arthur Hallam, the latter having brought from Italy a copy of the original pamphlet. The Cambridge edition, an octavo in paper wrappers, is now still scarcer than the Pisan one. The only other separate edition of *Adonais* was that of Mr. Buxton Forman, 1876, corresponding substantially with the form which the poem assumes in the *Complete Works of Shelley,* as produced by the same editor. It need hardly be said that *Adonais* was included in Mrs. Shelley's editions of her husband's Poems, and in all other editions of any fullness: it has also appeared in most of the volumes of Selections.

As early as 1830 there was an Italian translation of this Elegy. It is named *Adone, nella morte di Giovanni Keats, Elegia di Percy Bishe Shelley, tradotta da L. A.*

Damaso Pareto. Genova, dalla Tipografia Pellas, 1830. In this small quarto thirty pages are occupied by a notice of the life and poetry of Shelley.

I shall not here enter upon a consideration of the cancelled passages of ***Adonais*** : they will appear more appositely further on (see pp. 93-5, &c.). I therefore conclude the present section by quoting the ***Quarterly Review*** article upon ***Endymion*** —omitting only a few sentences which do not refer directly to Keats, but mostly to Leigh Hunt:—

'Reviewers have been sometimes accused of not reading the works which they affected to criticise. On the present occasion we shall anticipate the author's complaint, and honestly confess that we have not read his work. Not that we have been wanting in our duty; far from it; indeed, we have made efforts, almost as superhuman as the story itself appears to be, to get through it: but, with the fullest stretch of our perseverance, we are forced to confess that we have not been able to struggle beyond the first of the four books of which this Poetic Romance consists. We should extremely lament this want of energy, or whatever it may be, on our parts, were it not for one consolation—namely, that we are no better acquainted with the meaning of the book through which we have so painfully toiled than we are with that of the three which we have not looked into.

'It is not that Mr. Keats (if that be his real name, for we almost doubt that any man in his senses would put his real name to such a rhapsody)—it is not, we say, that the author has not powers of language, rays of fancy, and gleams of genius. He has all these: but he is unhappily a disciple of the new school of what has been somewhere called "Cockney Poetry," which may be defined to consist of the most incongruous ideas in the most uncouth language.

'Of this school Mr. Leigh Hunt, as we observed in a former number, aspires to be the hierophant. . . . This author is a copyist of Mr. Hunt: but he is more unintelligible, almost as rugged, twice as diffuse, and ten times more tiresome and absurd, than his prototype, who, though he impudently presumed to seat himself in the chair of criticism, and to measure his own poetry by his own standard, yet generally had a meaning. But Mr. Keats had advanced no dogmas which he was bound to support by examples. His nonsense, therefore, is quite gratuitous; he writes it for its own sake, and, being bitten by Mr. Leigh Hunt's insane criticism, more than rivals the insanity of his poetry.

'Mr. Keats's preface hints that his poem was produced under peculiar circumstances. "Knowing within myself," he says, "the manner in which this poem has been produced, it is not without a feeling of regret that I make it public. What manner I mean will be quite clear to the reader, who must soon perceive great inexperience, immaturity, and every error denoting a feverish attempt rather than a deed accomplished." We humbly beg his pardon, but this does not appear to us to be "quite so clear"; we really do not know what he means. But the next passage is more intelligible. "The two first books, and indeed the two last, I feel sensible, are not of such completion as to warrant their passing the press." Thus "the two first books" are, even in his own judgment, unfit to appear, and "the two last" are, it seems, in the same condition; and, as two and two make four, and as that is the whole number of books, we have a clear, and we believe a very just, estimate of the entire work.

'Mr. Keats, however, deprecates criticism on this "immature and feverish work" in terms which are themselves sufficiently feverish; and we confess that we should have abstained from inflicting upon him any of the tortures of the "fierce hell" of criticism [Footnote 1: The reader of Keats's Preface will find that this is a misrepresentation. Keats did not speak of any fierce hell of criticism, nor did he ask to remain uncriticized in order that he might write more. What he said was that a feeling critic would not fall foul of him for hoping to write good poetry in the long run, and would be aware that Keats's own sense of failure in Endymion was as fierce a hell as he could be chastised by.] which terrify his imagination if he had not begged to be spared in order that he might write more; if we had not observed in him a certain degree of talent which deserves to be put in the right way, or which at least ought to be warned of the wrong; and if finally he had not told us that he is of an age and temper which imperiously require mental discipline.

'Of the story we have been able to make out but little. It seems to be mythological, and probably relates to the loves of Diana and Endymion; but of this, as the scope of the work has altogether escaped us, we cannot speak with any degree of certainty, and must therefore content ourselves with giving some instances of its diction and versification. And here again we are perplexed and puzzled. At first it appeared to us that Mr. Keats had been amusing himself and wearying his readers with an immeasurable game at bouts rimés; *but, if we recollect rightly, it is an indispensable condition at this play that the rhymes, when filled up, shall have a meaning; and our author, as we have already hinted, has no meaning. He seems to us to write a line at random, and then he follows, not the thought excited by this line, but that suggested by the* rhyme with which it concludes. There is hardly a complete couplet enclosing a complete idea in the whole book. He wanders from one subject to another, from the association, not of ideas, but of sounds; and the work is composed of hemistichs which, it is quite evident, have forced themselves upon the author by the mere force of the catchwords on which they turn.

'We shall select, not as the most striking instance, but as that least liable to suspicion, a passage from the opening of the poem:—

"Such the sun, the moon,
Trees old and young, sprouting a shady boon
For simple sheep; and such are daffodils,
With the green world they live in; and clear rills
That for themselves a cooling covert make
'Gainst the hot season; the mid-forest brake
Rich with a sprinkling of fair musk-rose blooms;
And such too is the grandeur of the dooms
We have imagined for the mighty dead," &c.

Here it is clear that the word, and not the idea, *moon,* produces the simple sheep and their shady *boon,* and that "the *dooms* of the mighty dead" would never have intruded themselves but for the "fair musk-rose *blooms.*"

'Again:—

"For 'twas the morn. Apollo's upward fire
Made every eastern cloud a silvery pyre
Of brightness so unsullied that therein
A melancholy spirit well might win
Oblivion, and melt out his essence fine
Into the winds. Rain-scented eglantine
Gave temperate sweets to that well-wooing sun;
The lark was lost in him; cold springs had run
To warm their chilliest bubbles in the grass;
Man's voice was on the mountains; and the mass
Of Nature's lives and wonders pulsed tenfold
To feel this sunrise and its glories old."

Here Apollo's *fire* produces a *pyre* —a silvery pyre—of clouds, *wherein* a spirit might *win* oblivion, and melt his essence *fine;* and scented *eglantine* gives sweets to the *sun,* and cold springs had *run* into the *grass;* and then the pulse of the *mass* pulsed *tenfold* to feel the glories *old* of the new-born day, &c.

'One example more:—
"Be still the unimaginable lodge
For solitary thinkings, such as dodge
Conception to the very bourne of heaven,
Then leave the naked brain; be still the leaven
That, spreading in this dull and clodded earth,
Gives it a touch ethereal—a new birth."

Lodge, dodge—heaven, leaven—earth, birth —such, in six words, is the sum and substance of six lines.

'We come now to the author's taste in versification. He cannot indeed write a sentence, but perhaps he may be able to spin a line. Let us see. The following are specimens of his prosodial notions of our English heroic metre:—

"Dear as the temple's self, so does the moon,
The passion poesy, glories infinite.
"So plenteously all weed-hidden roots.
"Of some strange history, potent to send.
"Before the deep intoxication.
"Her scarf into a fluttering pavilion.
"The stubborn canvas for my voyage prepared.
"Endymion, the cave is secreter
Than the isle of Delos. Echo hence shall stir
No sighs but sigh-warm kisses, or light noise
Of thy combing hand, the while it travelling cloys
And trembles through my labyrinthine hair."

'By this time our readers must be pretty well satisfied as to the meaning of his sentences and the structure of his lines. We now present them with some of the new words with which, in imitation of Mr. Leigh Hunt, he adorns our language.

'We are told that turtles **passion** their voices; that an arbour was **nested,** and a lady's locks **gordianed** up; and, to supply the place of the nouns thus verbalized, Mr. Keats, with great fecundity, spawns new ones, such as men-slugs and human **serpentry,** the **honey-feel** of bliss, wives prepare **needments,** and so forth.

'Then he has formed new verbs by the process of cutting off their natural tails, the adverbs, and affixing them to their foreheads. Thus the wine out-sparkled, the multitude up-followed, and night up-took; the wind up-blows, and the hours are down-sunken. But, if he sinks some adverbs in the verbs, he compensates the language with adverbs and adjectives which he separates from the parent stock. Thus a lady whispers **pantingly** and close, makes **hushing** signs, and steers her skiff into a **ripply** cove, a shower falls **refreshfully,** and a vulture has a **spreaded** tail.

'But enough of Mr. Leigh Hunt and his simple neophyte. If any one should be bold enough to purchase this **Poetic Romance,** and so much more patient than ourselves as to get beyond the first book, and so much more fortunate as to find a meaning, we entreat him to make us acquainted with his success. We shall then return to the task which we now abandon in despair, and endeavour to make all due amends to Mr. Keats and to our readers.'

This criticism is not, I think, exactly what Shelley called it in the Preface to *Adonais* —'savage': it is less savage than contemptuous, and is far indeed from competing with the abuse which was from time to time, and in various reviews, poured forth upon Shelley himself. It cannot be denied that some of the blemishes which it points out in *Endymion* are real blemishes, and very serious ones. The grounds on which one can fairly object to the criticism are that its tone is purposely ill-natured; its recognition of merits scanty out of all proportion to its censure of defects; and its spirit that of prepense disparagement founded not so much on the poetical errors of Keats as on the fact that he was a friend of Leigh Hunt, the literary and also the political antagonist of the *Quarterly Review.* The Editor, Mr. Gifford, was long regarded as the author of this criticism; which is now known to have been written by Croker (*Memoir of John Murray,* i. 481, note).

That Keats was a friend of Leigh Hunt in the earlier period of his own poetical career is a fact; but not long after the appearance of the *Quarterly Review* article he conceived a good deal of dislike and even animosity against this literary ally. Possibly the taunts of the *Quarterly Review,* and the alienation of Keats from Hunt, had some connexion as cause and effect. In a letter from John Keats to his brother George and his sister-in-law occurs the following passage, [Footnote 1: This passage of the letter had remained unpublished up to 1890. It then appeared in Mr. Buxton Forman's volume, *Poetry and Prose by John Keats.* Some authentic information as to Keats's change of feeling had, however, been published before.], dated towards the end of 1818: 'Hunt has asked me to meet Tom Moore some day—so you shall hear of him. The night we went to Novello's there was a complete set-to of Mozart and punning. I was so completely tired of it that, if I were to follow my own inclinations, I should never meet any one of that set again; not even Hunt, who is certainly a pleasant fellow in the main, when you are with him—but in reality he is vain, egotistical, and disgusting in matters of taste, and in morals. He understands many a beautiful thing; but then, instead of giving other minds credit for the same degree of perception as he himself professes, he begins an explanation in such a curious manner that our taste and self-love are offended continually. Hunt does one harm by making fine things petty, and beautiful things hateful. Through him I am indifferent to Mozart, I care not for white busts; and many a glorious thing, when associated with him, becomes a nothing. This distorts one's mind—makes one's thoughts bizarre—perplexes one in the standard of Beauty.'

For the text of *Adonais* in the present edition I naturally have recourse to the original Pisan edition, but without neglecting such alterations as have been properly introduced into later issues: these will be fully indicated and accounted for in my Notes. In the minor matters of punctuation, &c. I do not consider myself bound to reproduce the first or any other edition, but I follow the plan which appears to myself most reasonable and correct; any point worthy of discussion in these details will also receive attention in the Notes.

ADONAIS:

ITS ARGUMENT

THE poem of *Adonais* can of course be contemplated from different points of view. Its biographical relations have been already considered in our preceding sections: its poetical structure and value, its ideal or spiritual significance, and its particular imagery and diction, will occupy us much as we proceed. At present I mean simply to deal with the Argument of *Adonais.* It has a thread—certainly a slender thread—of narrative or fable; the personation of the poetic figure *Adonais,* as distinct from the actual man John Keats, and the incidents with which that poetic figure is associated. The numerals which I put in parentheses indicate the stanzas in which the details occur.

(1) Adonais is now dead: the Hour which witnessed his loss mourns him, and

is to rouse the other Hours to mourn. (2) He was the son of the widowed Urania, (6) her youngest and dearest son. (2) He was slain by a nightly arrow—'pierced by the shaft which flies in darkness.' At the time of his death Urania was in her paradise (pleasure-garden), slumbering, while Echoes listened to the poems which he had written as death was impending. (3) Urania should now wake and weep; yet wherefore? 'He is gone where all things wise and fair descend.' (4) Nevertheless let her weep and lament. (7) Adonais had come to Rome. (8) Death and Corruption are now in his chamber, but Corruption delays as yet to strike. (9) The Dreams whom he nurtured, as a herdsman tends his flock, mourn around him. (10) One of them was deceived for a moment into supposing that a tear shed by itself came from the eyes of Adonais, and must indicate that he was still alive, (11) Another washed his limbs, and a third clipped and shed her locks upon his corpse, &c. (13) Then came others—Desires, Adorations, Fantasies, &c. (14 to 16) Morning lamented, and Echo, and Spring. (17) Albion wailed. May 'the curse of Cain light on his head who pierced thy innocent breast,' and scared away its angel soul! (20) Can it be that the soul alone dies, when nothing else is annihilated? (22) Misery aroused Urania: urged by Dreams and Echoes, she sprang up, and (23) sought the death-chamber of Adonais, (24) enduring much suffering from 'barbed tongues, and thoughts more sharp than they.' (25) As she arrived, Death was shamed for a moment, and Adonais breathed again: but immediately afterwards 'Death rose and smiled, and met her vain caress.' (26) Urania would fain have died along with Adonais; but, chained as she was to Time, this was denied her. (27) She reproached Adonais for having, though defenceless, dared the dragon in his den. Had he waited till the day of his maturity, 'the monsters of life's waste' would have fled from him, as (28) the wolves, ravens, and vultures had fled from, and fawned upon, 'the Pythian of the age.' (30) Then came the Mountain Shepherds, bewailing Adonais: the Pilgrim of Eternity, the Lyrist of Ierne, and (31) among others, one frail form, a pard-like spirit. (34) Urania asked the name of this last Shepherd: he then made bare his branded and ensanguined brow, which was like Cain's or Christ's. (35) Another Mountain Shepherd, 'the gentlest of the wise,' leaned over the deathbed. (36) Adonais has drunk poison. Some 'deaf and viperous murderer' gave him the envenomed draught.

[I must here point out a singular discrepancy in the poem of *Adonais,* considered as a narrative or apologue. Hitherto we had been told that Adonais was killed by an arrow or dart—he was 'pierced by the shaft which flies in darkness,' and the man who 'pierced his innocent breast' had incurred the curse of Cain: he had 'a wound' (stanza 22). There was also the alternative statement that Adonais, un-equipped with the shield of wisdom or the spear of scorn, had been so rash as to 'dare the unpastured dragon in his den'; and from this the natural inference is that not any 'shaft which flies in darkness,' but the dragon himself, had slaughtered the too-venturous youth. But now we hear that he was done to death by poison. Certainly, when we look beneath the symbol into the thing symbolized, we can see that these divergent allegations represent the same fact, and the readers of the Elegy are not called upon to form themselves into a coroner's jury to determine whether a 'shaft' or a 'dragon' or 'poison' was the instrument of murder: nevertheless the statements in the text are neither identical nor reconcileable for purposes of mythical narra-tion, and it seems strange that the author should not have taken this into account. It will be found as we proceed (see p. 70) that the reference to 'poison' comes into the poem as a direct reproduction from the Elegy of Moschus upon Bion—being the passage which forms the second of the two mottoes to *Adonais.*]

(36) This murderer, a 'nameless worm,' was alone callous to the prelude of the forthcoming song. (37) Let him live on in remorse and self-contempt. (38) Neither should we weep that Adonais has 'fled far from these carrion-kites that scream be-low.' His spirit flows back to its fountain, a portion of the Eternal. (39) Indeed, he is not dead nor sleeping, but 'has awakened from the dream of life.' Not he decays, but we. (41) Let not us, nor the powers of Nature, mourn for Adonais. (42) He is made one with Nature. (45) In 'the unapparent' he was welcomed by Chatterton, Sidney, Lucan, and (46) many more immortals, and was hailed as the master of a 'kingless sphere' in a 'heaven of song.' (48) Let any rash mourner go to Rome, and (49) visit the cemetery. (53) And thou, my heart, why linger and shrink? Adonais calls thee: be no longer divided from him. (55) The soul of Adonais beacons to thee 'from the abode where the Eternal are.'

This may be the most convenient place for raising a question of leading im-portance to the Argument of *Adonais* —Who is the personage designated under the name Urania?—a question which, so far as I know, has never yet been mooted among the students of Shelley. Who is Urania? Why is she represented as the mother of Adonais (Keats), and the chief mourner for his untimely death?

In mythology the word Urania has two distinct applications. It is the name of one of the nine Muses (Hesiod, *Theog.* 78), to whom in later times Astronomy is assigned as a special province. As an adjective it is attached to Aphrodite in one of her aspects (**Herodotus,** i. 105, iv. 59, &c.); and Plato in the **Banquet,** a dialogue translated by Shelley (begun in 1818), lays much stress upon the distinction between the elder-born Aphrodite Urania, the motherless daughter of Heaven, and Aphrodite Pandemos (the Common), daughter of Zeus and Dione. The fragmentary poem of Shelley named **Prince Athanase,** written in 1817, was at first named **Pandemos and Urania,** and was intended, as Mrs. Shelley informs us, to embody the contrast between 'the earthly and unworthy Venus,' and the nobler ideal of love, the heaven-born or heaven-sent Venus. The poem would thus have borne a certain relation to **Alastor,** and also to **Epipsychidion.** The use of the name 'Urania' in this proposed title may help to confirm us in the belief that there is no reason why Shelley should not have used the same name in **Adonais,** with the implied meaning of Aphrodite Urania.

If the personage in Shelley's Elegy is to be regarded, not as the Muse Urania, but as Aphrodite Urania, she here represents spiritual or intellectual aspiration, the love of abstract beauty, the divine element in poesy or art. As such, Aphrodite Urania would be no less appropriate than Urania or any other Muse to be designated as the mother of Adonais (Keats). But the more cogent argument in favour of Aphrodite Urania is to be based upon grounds of analogy or transfer, rather than upon any reason of antecedent probability. The part assigned to Urania in Shelley's Elegy is very closely modelled upon the part assigned to Aphrodite in the Elegy of Bion upon Adonis (see the section in this volume, **Bion and Moschus**). What Aphrodite Cypris does in the **Adonis,** that Urania does in the **Adonais.** The resemblances are exceedingly close, in substance and in detail: the divergences are only such as the altered conditions naturally dictate. The Cyprian Aphrodite is the bride of Adonis, and as such she bewails him: the Uranian Aphrodite is the mother of Adonais, and she laments him accordingly. Carnal relationship and carnal love are transposed into spiritual relationship and spiritual love. The hands are the hands, in both poems, of Aphrodite: the voices are respectively those of Cypris and of Urania.

On the whole I am strongly of opinion that the Urania of **Adonais** is Aphrodite, and not the Muse.

On the other hand, it is to be observed that Urania is first mentioned in close connexion with Milton. The 'most musical of mourners' is still mourning the loss of her great elder-born son, and is now called to mourn her 'youngest, dearest one'; just as the Meles, 'most musical of rivers,' who of old lost Homer, is said in Moschus's Elegy for Bion to weep for another son, wasting away in a new sorrow. Many readers will recollect that Milton, in the elaborate address which opens Book VII of **Paradise Lost,** invokes Urania. He is careful however to say that he does not mean the Muse Urania, but the spirit of 'Celestial Song,' sister of Eternal Wisdom, both of them well-pleasing to the 'Almighty Father,' in fact the 'Heavenly Muse' of the opening of Book I. It can hardly be but that some recollection of this 'Heavenly Muse' was in Shelley's mind, and was meant to be suggested to his readers, even though the primary reference be to Aphrodite the Heavenly.

On the supposition that Urania the Muse is referred to, a subordinate point of some difficulty arises from stanza 6, where Adonais is spoken of as 'the nursling of thy widowhood'—which seems to mean, son of Urania, born after the father's death. Urania the Muse is credited in mythology with the motherhood of two sons—Linus, her offspring by Amphimarus, who was a son of Poseidon, and Hymenaeus, her offspring by Apollo. It might be idle to puzzle over this question of Urania's 'widowhood,' or to attempt to found upon it any theory as to who her deceased consort could have been: for it is as likely as not that the phrase which I have cited from the poem is not intended to define with any sort of precision the parentage of the supposititious Adonais, but, practically ignoring Adonais, applies to Keats himself, and means simply that Keats, as the son of the Muse, was born out of time—born in an unpoetical and unappreciative age. It would also be according to the analogy of Greek and Latin to use 'widowhood' of bereavement generally, here of the bereavement caused to Urania by the death of Milton. Compare Heber's 'Mourn, widowed Queen.'

If we were to suppose (but I have already discarded the supposition) that the Urania of Adonais is truly the Muse, and if we regard this Muse as specially the Muse of Astronomy, we might ask—why should Shelley have selected the Muse of Astronomy, above all others, for the motherhood of Keats? Keats never wrote about astronomy, and had no qualifications and no faintest inclination for writing about it: this science, and every other exact or speculative science, were highly alien from his disposition and turn of mind. And yet, on casting about for a reason, we can find that after all and in a certain sense there is one forthcoming, of some considerable amount of relevancy. In the eyes of Shelley, Keats was principally and above all the poet of **Hyperion** : and **Hyperion** is, strictly speaking, a poem about the sun. In like manner, **Endymion** is a poem about the moon. Thus, from one point of view—I cannot see any other—Keats might be regarded as inspired by, or a son of, the Muse of Astronomy. But I only make this remark by the way, as it leaves the main argument quite unaffected.

ADONAIS:

GENERAL EXPOSITION

THE consideration which, in the preceding section, we have bestowed upon the 'Argument' of **Adonais** will assist us not a little in grasping the full scope of the poem. It may be broadly divided into three currents of thought, or (as one might say) into three acts of passion. 1. The sense of grievous loss in the death of John Keats the youthful and aspiring poet, cut short as he was approaching his prime; and the instinctive impulse to mourning, and desolation. 2. The mythical or symbolic embodiment of the events in the laments of Urania and the Mountain Shepherds, and in the denunciation of the ruthless destroyer of the peace and life of Adonais. 3. The rejection of mourning as one-sided, ignorant, and a reversal of the true estimate of the facts; and a recognition of the eternal destiny of Keats in the world of mind, coupled with the yearning of Shelley to have done with the vain shows of things in this cycle of mortality, and to be at one with Keats in the mansions of the everlasting. Such is the evolution of this Elegy; from mourning to rapture: from a purblind consideration of deathly phenomena to the illumination of the individual spirit which contemplates the eternity of spirit as the universal substance.

Shelley raises in his poem a very marked contrast between the death of Adonais (Keats) as a mortal man succumbing to 'the common fate,' and the immortality of his spirit as a vital immaterial essence surviving the death of the body: he uses terms such as might be adopted by any believer in the doctrine of 'the immortality of the soul,' in the ordinary sense of that phrase. It would not however be safe to infer that Shelley, at the precise time when he wrote *Adonais,* was really in a more definite frame of mind on this theme than at other periods of his life, or of a radically different conviction. As a fact, his feelings on the great problems of immortality were acute, his opinions regarding them vague and unsettled. He certainly was not an adherent of the typical belief on this subject: the belief that a man on this earth is a combination of body and soul, in a state—his sole state—of 'probation'; that, when the body dies and decays, the soul continues to be the same absolute individual identity; and that it passes into a condition of eternal and irreversible happiness of misery, according to the irreversible happiness or misery, according to the faith entertained or the deeds done in the body. His belief amounted more nearly to this: That a human soul is a portion of the Universal Soul, subjected, during its connexion with the body, to all the illusions, the dreams and nightmares, of sense; and that, after the death of the body, it continues to be a portion of the Universal Soul, liberated from those illusions, and subsisting in some condition which the human reason is not capable of defining as a state either of personal consciousness or of absorption. And, so far as the human being exercised, during the earthly life, the authentic functions of soul, that same exercise of function continues to be the permanent record of the soul in the world of mind. If any reader thinks that this seems a vague form of belief, the answer is that the belief of Shelley was indeed a vague one. In the poem of *Adonais* it remains, to my apprehension, as vague as in his other writings: but it assumes a shape of greater definition, because the poem is, by its scheme and intent, a personating poem, in which the soul of Keats has to be greeted by the soul of Chatterton, just as the body of Adonais has to be caressed and bewailed by Urania. Using language of a semi-emblematic kind, we might perhaps express something of Shelley's belief thus:—Mankind is the microcosm, as distinguished from the rest of the universe, which forms the macrocosm; and, as long as a man's body and soul remain in combination, his soul pertains to the microcosm: when this combination ceases with the death of the body, his soul, in whatever sense it may be held to exist, lapses into the macrocosm, but there is neither knowledge as to the mode of its existence, nor speech capable of recording this.

As illustrating our poet's conceptions on these mysterious subjects, I append extracts from three of his prose writings. The first extract comes from his fragment **On Life,** which may have been written (but this is quite uncertain) towards 1815; the second from his fragment **On a Future State,** for which some similar date is suggested; the third from the notes to his drama of **Hellas,** written in 1821, later than **Adonais.**

(1) 'The most refined abstractions of logic conduct to a view of Life which, though startling to the apprehension, is in fact that which the habitual sense of its repeated combinations has extinguished in us. It strips, as it were, the painted curtain from this scene of things. I confess that I am one of those who am unable to refuse my assent [Footnote 1: This phrase is lumbering and not grammatical. The words 'I confess that I am unable to refuse' would be all that the meaning requires.] to the conclusions of those philosophers who assert that nothing exists but as it is perceived. It is a decision against which all our persuasions struggle—and we must be long convicted before we can be convinced that the solid universe of external things is "such stuff as dreams are made of." The shocking absurdities of the popular philosophy of mind and matter, its fatal consequences in morals, and their [? the] violent dogmatism concerning the source of all things, had early conducted me to Materialism. This Materialism is a seducing system to young and superficial minds: it allows its disciples to talk, and dispenses them from thinking. But I was discontented with such a view of things as it afforded. Man is a being of high aspirations, "looking both before and after," whose "thoughts wander through eternity," disclaiming alliance with transience and decay; incapable of imagining to himself

annihilation; existing but in the future and the past; being, not what he is, but what he has been and shall be. Whatever may be his true and final destination, there is a spirit within him at enmity with nothingness and dissolution. This is the character of all life and being. Each is at once the centre and the circumference; the point to which all things are referred, and the line in which all things are contained. Such contemplations as these Materialism, and the popular philosophy of mind and matter, alike forbid: they are only consistent with the Intellectual System. . . . The view of Life presented by the most refined deductions of the Intellectual Philosophy is that of unity. Nothing exists but as it is perceived. The difference is merely nominal between those two classes of thought which are vulgarly distinguished by the names of "ideas" and of "external objects." Pursuing the same thread of reasoning, the existence of distinct individual minds, similar to that which is employed in now questioning its own nature, is likewise found to be a delusion. The words "I, you, they," are not signs of any actual difference subsisting between the assemblage of thoughts thus indicated, but are merely marks employed to denote the different modifications of the one mind. Let it not be supposed that this doctrine conducts to the monstrous presumption that I, the person who now write and think, am that one mind. I am but a portion of it.'

(2) 'Suppose however that the intellectual and vital principle differs in the most marked and essential manner from all other known substances; that they have all some resemblance between themselves which *it* in no degree participates. In what manner can this concession be made an argument for its imperishability? All that we see or know perishes [Footnote 1: This seems to contradict the phrase in *Adonais* (stanza 20) 'Nought we know dies.' Probably Shelley, in the prose passage, does not intend 'perishes' to be accepted in the absolute sense of 'dies,' or 'ceases to have any existence:' he means that all things undergo a process of deterioration and decay, leading on to some essential change or transmutation. The French have the word 'dépérir' as well as 'périr': Shelley's 'perishes' would correspond to 'dépérit.'] and is changed. Life and thought differ indeed from everything else: but that it survives that period beyond which we have no experience of its existence such distinction and dissimilarity affords no shadow of proof, and nothing but our own desires could have led us to conjecture or imagine. Have we existed before birth? It is difficult

to conceive the possibility of this. . . . If we have ***not*** existed before birth; if, at the period when the parts of our nature on which thought and life depend seem to be woven together, they ***are*** woven together; if there are no reasons to suppose that we have existed before that period at which our existence apparently commences; then there are no grounds for supposition that we shall continue to exist after our existence has apparently ceased. So far as thought and life is concerned, the same will take place with regard to us, individually considered, after death, as had place before our birth. It is said that it is possible that we should continue to exist in some mode totally inconceivable to us at present. This is a most unreasonable presumption. . . . Such assertions . . . persuade indeed only those who desire to be persuaded. This desire to be for ever as we are—the reluctance to a violent and unexperienced change which is common to all the animated and inanimate combinations of the universe—is indeed the secret persuasion which has given birth to the opinions of a Future State.'

(3.) Note to the chorus, 'Worlds on worlds are rolling ever,' &c.) 'The first stanza contrasts the immortality of the living and thinking beings which inhabit the planets and (to use a common and inadequate phrase) clothe themselves in matter, with the transience of the noblest manifestations of the external world. The concluding verses indicate a progressive state of more or less exalted existence, according to the degree of perfection which every distinct intelligence may have attained. Let it not be supposed that I mean to dogmatise upon a subject concerning which all men are equally ignorant, or that I think the Gordian knot of the origin of evil can be disentangled by that or any similar assertions. . . . That there is a true solution of the riddle, and that in our present state that solution is unattainable by us, are propositions which may be regarded as equally certain: meanwhile, as it is the province of the poet to attach himself to those ideas which exalt and ennoble humanity, let him be permitted to have conjectured the condition of that futurity towards which we are all impelled by an inextinguishable thirst for immortality. Until better arguments can be produced than sophisms which disgrace the cause, this desire itself must remain the strongest and the only presumption that eternity is the inheritance of every thinking being.'

The reader will perceive that in these three passages the dominant ideas, very briefly stated, are as follows:—(1) Mind is the aggregate of all individual minds; (2) man has no reason for expecting that his mind or soul will be immortal; (3) no reason, except such as inheres in the very desire which he feels for immortality. These opinions, deliberately expressed by Shelley at different dates as a theorist in prose, should be taken into account if we endeavour to estimate what he means when, as a poet, he speaks, whether in **Hellas** or in **Adonais,** of an individual, his mind and his immortality. When Shelley calls upon us to regard Keats (Adonais) as mortal in body but immortal in soul or mind, his real intent is probably limited to this: that Keats has been liberated, by the death of the body, from the dominion and delusions of the senses; and that he, while in the flesh, developed certain fruits of mind which survive his body, and will continue to survive it indefinitely, and will form a permanent inheritance of thought and of beauty to succeeding generations. Keats himself, in one of his most famous lines, expressed a like conception—

'A thing of beauty is a joy for ever.'

Shelley was faithful to his canons of highest literary or poetical form in giving a Greek shape to his Elegy on Keats: but it may be allowed to his English readers, or at any rate to some of them, to think that he hereby fell into a certain degree of artificiality of structure, undesirable in itself, and more especially hampering him in a plain and self-consistent expression both of his real feeling concerning Keats, and of his resentment against those who had cut short, or were supposed to have cut short, the career and the poetical work of his friend. Moreover Shelley went beyond the mere recurrence to Greek forms of impersonation and expression: he took two particular Greek authors, and two particular Greek poems, as his principal model. These two poems are the Elegy of Bion on Adonis, and the Elegy of Moschus on Bion. To imitate is not to plagiarize; and Shelley cannot reasonably be called a plagiarist because he introduced into **Adonais** passages which are paraphrased or even translated from Bion and Moschus. It does seem singular however that neither in the **Adonais** volume nor in any of his numerous written remarks upon the poem does Shelley ever once refer to this state of the facts. Possibly in using the name 'Adonais' he intended to refer the reader indirectly to the 'Adonis' of Bion;

and he prefixed to the preface of his poem, as a motto, four verses from the Elegy of Moschus upon Bion. This may have been intended for a hint to the reader as to the Grecian sources of the poem. The whole matter will receive detailed treatment in our next section, as well as in the Notes.

The passages of *Adonais* which can be traced back to Bion and Moschus are not the finest things in the poem: mostly they fill out its fabular 'argument' with brilliancy and suavity, rather than with nerve and pathos. The finest things are to be found in the denunciation of the 'deaf and viperous murderer'; in the stanzas concerning the 'Mountain Shepherds,' especially the figure representing Shelley himself; and in the solemn and majestic conclusion, where the poet rises from the region of earthly sorrow into the realm of ideal aspiration and contemplation.

Shelley is generally—and I think most justly—regarded as a peculiarly melodious versifier: but it must not be supposed that he is rigidly exact in his use of rhyme. The contrary can be proved from the entire body of his poems. *Adonais* is, in this respect, neither more nor less correct than his other writings. It would hardly be reasonable to attribute his laxity in rhyming to either carelessness, indifference, or unskilfulness: but rather to a deliberate preference for a certain variety in the rhyme-sounds—as tending to please the ear, and availing to satisfy it in the total effect, without cloying it by any tight-drawn uniformity. Such a preference can be justified on two grounds: firstly, that the general effect of the slightly varied sounds is really the more gratifying of the two methods, and I believe that, practised within reasonable limits, it is so; and secondly, that the requirements of sense are superior to those of sound, and that, in the effort after severely exact rhyming, a writer would often be compelled to sacrifice some delicacy of thought, or some grace or propriety of diction. Looking through the stanzas of *Adonais,* I find the following laxities of rhyming: Compeers, dares; anew, knew (this repetition of an identical syllable as if it were a rhyme is very frequent with Shelley, who evidently considered it to be permissible, and even right—and in this view he has plenty of support); God, road; last, waste; taught, not; break, cheek (two instances); ground, moaned; both, youth; rise, arise; song, stung; steel, fell; light, delight; part, depart; wert, heart; wrong, tongue; brow, so; moan, one; crown, tone; song, unstrung; knife, grief; mourn, burn;

dawn, moan; bear, bear; blot, thought; renown, Chatterton; thought, not; approved, reproved; forth, earth; nought, not; home, tomb; thither, together; wove, of; riven, heaven. These are 34 instances of irregularity. The number of stanzas in *Adonais* is 55: therefore there is more than one such irregularity for every two stanzas.

It may not be absolutely futile if we bestow a little more attention upon the details of these laxities of rhyme. The repetition of an identical syllable has been cited 6 times. In 4 instances the sound of *taught* is assimilated to that of *not* (I take here no account of differences of spelling, but only of the sounds); in 4, the sound of *ground* and of *renown* to that of *moaned,* or of *Chatterton;* in 2, the sound of *o* in *road, both,* and *wove,* to that in *God, youth,* and *of;* in 3, the sound of *song* to that of *stung;* in 2, the sound of *ee* in *compeers, steel, cheek,* and *grief,* to the sound in *dares, fell, break,* and *knife;* in 2, the sound of *e* in *wert* and *earth* to that in *heart* and *forth;* in 3, the sound of *o* in *moan* and *home* to that in *one, dawn,* and *tomb;* in 2, the sound of *thither* to that of *together.* The other cases which I have cited have only a single instance apiece. It results therefore that the vowel-sound subjected to the most frequent variations is that of *o,* whether single or in combination.

Shelley may be considered to allow himself more than an average degree of latitude in rhyming: but it is a fact that, if the general body of English poetry is scrutinized, it will be found to be more or less lax in this matter. This question is complicated by another question—that of how words were pronounced at different periods in our literary history: in order to exclude the most serious consequent difficulties, I shall say nothing here about any poet prior to Milton. I take at haphazard four pages of rhymed verse from each of the following six poets, and the result proves to be as follows:—

Milton. —Pass, was; feast, rest; come, room; still, invisible; vouchsafe, safe; moon, whereon; ordained, land. 7 instances.

Dryden. —Alone, fruition; guard, heard; pursued, good; procured, secured. 4

instances.

Pope. —Given, heaven; steer, character; board, lord; fault, thought; err, singular. 5 instances.

Gray. —Beech, stretch; borne, thorn; abode, God; broke, rock. 4 instances.

Coleridge. —Not a single instance.

Byron. —Given, heaven; Moore, yore; look, duke; song, tongue; knot, not; of, enough; bestowed, mood. 7 instances.

In all these cases, as in that of Shelley's *Adonais,* I have taken no count of those instances of lax sound-rhyme which are correct letter-rhyme—such as the coupling of *move* with *love,* or of *star* with *war;* for these, however much some more than commonly purist ears may demur to them, appear to be part and parcel of the rhyming system of the English language. I need hardly say that, if these cases had been included, my list would in every instance have swelled considerably; nor yet that I am conscious how extremely partial and accidental is the test, as to comparative number of laxities, which I have here supplied.

The 'Spenserian stanza,' in which the *Adonais* is written, was devised by Spenser as a vehicle proper for the expression of the romantic themes of the *Faery Queen.* In the *Shepherd's Calendar* he had used Chaucer's eight-lined stanza in which the rhymes run *ababbcbc.* To this stanza Spenser now added, as a ninth line, an Alexandrine or twelve-syllable line, rhyming with the sixth and eighth lines, thus *ababbcbcc;* and so obtained some of the effect of the *Ottava rima* used by Ariosto and Tasso, *abababcc,* where the close of each strophe is marked by the rhyme of its two last lines. Warton (Todd's *Spenser,* ii. p. cxxvi) criticizes Spenser's invention as showing an imperfect feeling for the genius of the English language, and leading the poet into redundances and ellipses of expression, and also into false or strained rhymes. On the other hand he allows that 'the fullness and significancy of Spenser's descriptions is often owing to the prolixity of his stanza, and the multitude of his rhymes.' The stanza was successfully used by Thomson in the *Castle of Indolence,* and by Beattie in the *Minstrel.* Byron, in his preface to the First and Second Cantos of *Childe Harold* (1812), writes:—

'The stanza of Spenser, according to one of our most successful poets, admits of every variety. Dr. Beattie makes the following observation:—"Not long ago, I began a poem in the style and stanza of Spenser, in which I propose to give full scope to my inclination, and be either droll or pathetic, descriptive or sentimental, tender or satirical, as the humour strikes me; for, if I mistake not, the measure which I have adopted admits equally of all these kinds of composition."'

Shelley had employed it in the *Revolt of Islam* (1817) (not to speak of his juvenile Poems by Margaret Nicholson), and he says:—

'I have adopted the stanza of Spenser (a measure inexpressibly beautiful) not because I consider it a finer model of poetical harmony than the blank verse of Shakespeare and Milton, but because in the latter there is no shelter for mediocrity: you must either succeed or fail. This perhaps an aspiring spirit should desire. But I was enticed also by the brilliancy and magnificence of sound which a mind that has been nourished upon musical thoughts can produce by a just and harmonious arrangement of the pauses of this measure.'

As is here pointed out, the metre admits of great variety, according to the incidence of the pause. The metrical structure of the first two cantos of *Childe Harold* is more even and regular than that of the later parts of the poem. The versification of the *Adonais* appears to be more matured than that of the *Revolt of Islam;* and 'weak,' or double rhymes, are very sparingly used.

The metre has been used by the late Mr. Philip Worsley for his translations of the *Odyssey* and *Iliad,* and has stood the severe test successfully. It has also been used by Mr. George Musgrave (1893) in a translation of Dante's *Inferno.* This was a bold experiment, but not exactly an unreasonable one, as the chief pauses of Dante's own metre often fall naturally on the ninth line.

See Courthope's *History of English Poetry,* vol. ii. p. 279; also Tozer's *Childe Harold,* Clarendon Press, 1885.

BION AND MOSCHUS

The relation of Shelley's Elegy of *Adonais* to the two Elegies written by Bion and by Moschus must no doubt have been observed, and been more or less remarked upon, as soon as *Adonais* obtained some currency among classical readers; Captain Medwin, in his *Shelley Papers,* 1832, referred to it. I am not however aware that the resemblances had ever been brought out in detail until Mr. G. S. D. Murray, of Christ Church, Oxford, noted down the passages from Bion, which were published accordingly in my edition of Shelley's Poems, 1870. Since then, in 1888, Lieut.-Colonel Hime, R.A., issued a pamphlet (Dulau & Co.) entitled *The Greek Materials of Shelley's Adonais, with Remarks on the three Great English Elegies,* entering into further, yet not exhaustive, particulars on the same subject. Shelley himself made a fragmentary translation from the Elegy of Bion on Adonis: it was first printed in Mr. Forman's edition of Shelley's Poems, 1877. I append here those passages which are directly related to *Adonais* :—

'I mourn Adonis dead—loveliest Adonis—
Dead, dead Adonis—and the Loves lament.
Sleep no more, Venus, wrapped in purple woof—
Wake, violet-stolèd queen, and weave the crown
Of death,—'tis Misery calls,—for he is dead.
. . . . Aphrodite
With hair unbound is wandering through the woods,
Wildered, ungirt, unsandalled—the thorns pierce

Her hastening feet, and drink her sacred blood.

The flowers are withered up with grief.

Echo resounds, . . "Adonis dead!"

She clasped him, and cried . . "Stay, Adonis!
Stay, dearest one, . .
And mix my lips with thine!
Wake yet a while, Adonis—oh but once!—
That I may kiss thee now for the last time—
But for as long as one short kiss may live!"'

The reader familiar with **Adonais** will recognize the passages in that poem of which we here have the originals. To avoid repetition, I do not cite them at the moment, but shall call attention to them successively in my Notes at the end of the volume.

For other passages, also utilized by Shelley, I have recourse to the volume of Mr. Andrew Lang (Macmillan & Co. 1889), ***Theocritus, Bion, and Moschus, rendered into English Prose.*** And first, from Bion's Elegy on Adonis:—

'The flowers flush red for anguish. . . . This kiss will I treasure, even as thyself, Adonis, since, ah ill-fated! thou art fleeing me, . . . while wretched I yet live, being a goddess, and may not follow thee. Persephone, take thou my lover, my lord, for thyself art stronger than I, and all lovely things drift down to thee. . . . For why, ah overbold! didst thou follow the chase, and, being so fair, why wert thou thus over-hardy to fight with beasts? . . . A tear the Paphian sheds for each blood-drop of Adonis, and tears and blood on the earth are turned to flowers. . . . Ah even in death he is beautiful, beautiful in death, as one that hath fallen on sleep. . . . All things have perished in his death, yea all the flowers are faded. . . . He reclines, the delicate Adonis, in his raiment of purple, and around him the Loves are weeping and groaning aloud, clipping their locks for Adonis. And one upon his shafts, another on his bow, is treading, and one hath loosed the sandal of Adonis, and another hath broken his own feathered quiver, and one in a golden vessel bears water, and another laves the wound, and another, from behind him, with his wings is fanning Adonis. . . . Thou must again bewail him, again must weep for him another year. . . .

He does not heed them [the Muses]; not that he is loth to hear, but that the Maiden of Hades doth not let him go.'

The next-ensuing passages come from the Elegy of Moschus for Bion:—

'Ye flowers, now in sad clusters breathe yourselves away. Now redden, ye roses, in your sorrow, and now wax red, ye wind-flowers; now, thou hyacinth, whisper the letters on thee graven, and add a deeper ai ai to thy petals: he is dead, the beautiful singer. . . . Ye nightingales that lament among the thick leaves of the trees, tell ye to the Sicilian waters of Arethusa the tidings that Bion the herdsman is dead. . . . Thy sudden doom, O Bion, Apollo himself lamented, and the Satyrs mourned thee, and the Priapi in sable raiment, and the Panes sorrow for thy song, and the Fountain-fairies in the wood made moan, and their tears turned to rivers of waters. And Echo in the rocks laments that thou art silent, and no more she mimics thy voice. And in sorrow for thy fall the trees cast down their fruit, and all the flowers have faded. . . . Nor ever sang so sweet the nightingale on the cliffs, . . . nor so much, by the grey sea-waves, did ever the sea-bird sing, nor so much in the dells of dawn did the bird of Memnon bewail the son of the Morning, fluttering around his tomb, as they lamented for Bion dead. . . . Echo, among the reeds, doth still feed upon thy songs. . . . This, O most musical of rivers, is thy second sorrow,—this, Meles, thy new woe. Of old didst thou lose Homer: . . . now again another son thou weepest, and in a new sorrow art thou wasting away. . . . Nor so much did pleasant Lesbos mourn for Alcaeus, nor did the Teian town so greatly bewail her poet, . . . and not for Sappho but still for thee doth Mitylene wail her musical lament. . . . Ah me! when the mallows wither in the garden, and the green parsley, and the curled tendrils of the anise, on a later day they live again, and spring in another year: but we men, we the great and mighty or wise, when once we have died, in hollow earth we sleep, gone down into silence. . . . Poison came, Bion, to thy mouth—thou didst know poison. To such lips as thine did it come, and was not sweetened? What mortal was so cruel that could mix poison for thee, or who could give thee the venom that heard thy voice? Surely he had no music in his soul. . . . But justice hath overtaken them all.'

Bion was born in Smyrna, or in a neighbouring village named Phlossa, and may have died at some date not far from 250 B. C. The statement of Moschus that Bion was poisoned by certain enemies appears to be intended as an assertion of actual fact Of Moschus nothing distinct is known, beyond his being a native of Sicily.

ADONAIS;
AN ELEGY ON THE DEATH OF JOHN KEATS,

Author of *Endymion, Hyperion,* &c.

PLATO.

PREFACE.

MOSCHUS, EPITAPH. BION.

IT is my intention to subjoin to the London edition of this poem a criticism upon the claims of its lamented object to be classed among the writers of the highest genius who have adorned our age. My known repugnance to the narrow principles of taste on which several of his earlier compositions were modelled proves at least that I am an impartial judge. I consider the fragment of *Hyperion* as second to nothing that was ever produced by a writer of the same years.

John Keats died at Rome of a consumption, in his twenty-fourth year, on the [23rd] of [February] 1821; and was buried in the romantic and lonely cemetery of the protestants in that city, under the pyramid which is the tomb of Cestius, and the massy walls and towers, now mouldering and desolate, which formed the circuit of ancient Rome. The cemetery is an open space among the ruins, covered in winter with violets and daisies. It might make one in love with death to think that one should be buried in so sweet a place.

The genius of the lamented person to whose memory I have dedicated these unworthy verses was not less delicate and fragile than it was beautiful; and where canker-worms abound what wonder if its young flower was blighted in the bud? The savage criticism on his *Endymion* which appeared in the *Quarterly Review* produced the most violent effect on his susceptible mind; the agitation thus originated ended in the rupture of a blood-vessel in the lungs; a rapid consumption ensued; and the succeeding acknowledgments, from more candid critics, of the true greatness of his powers, were ineffectual to heal the wound thus wantonly inflicted.

It may be well said that these wretched men know not what they do. They scatter their insults and their slanders without heed as to whether the poisoned shaft lights on a heart made callous by many blows, or one, like Keats's, composed of more penetrable stuff. One of their associates is, to my knowledge, a most base and unprincipled calumniator. As to *Endymion,* was it a poem, whatever might be its defects, to be treated contemptuously by those who had celebrated with various degrees of complacency and panegyric *Paris,* and *Woman,* and *A Syrian Tale,* and Mrs. Lefanu, and Mr. Barrett, and Mr. Howard Payne, and a long list of the illustrious obscure? Are these the men who, in their venal good-nature, presumed to draw a parallel between the Rev. Mr. Milman and Lord Byron? What gnat did they strain at here, after having swallowed all those camels? Against what woman taken in adultery dares the foremost of these literary prostitutes to cast his opprobrious stone? Miserable man! you, one of the meanest, have wantonly defaced one of the noblest specimens of the workmanship of God. Nor shall it be your excuse that, murderer as you are, you have spoken daggers, but used none.

The circumstances of the closing scene of poor Keats's life were not made known to me until the Elegy was ready for the press. I am given to understand that the wound which his sensitive spirit had received from the criticism of *Endymion* was exasperated by the bitter sense of unrequited benefits; the poor fellow seems to have been hooted from the stage of life, no less by those on whom he had wasted the promise of his genius than those on whom he had lavished his fortune and his care. He was accompanied to Rome, and attended in his last illness, by Mr. Severn, a young artist of the highest promise, who, I have been informed, 'almost risked his own life, and sacrificed every prospect to unwearied attendance upon his dying friend.' Had I known these circumstances before the completion of my poem, I should have been tempted to add my feeble tribute of applause to the more solid recompense which the virtuous man finds in the recollection of his own motives. Mr. Severn can dispense with a reward from 'such stuff as dreams are made of.' His conduct is a golden augury of the success of his future career. May the unextinguished Spirit of his illustrious friend animate the creations of his pencil, and plead against oblivion for his name!

ADONAIS

1

I WEEP for Adonais—he is dead!
Oh weep for Adonais, though our tears
Thaw not the frost which binds so dear a head!
And thou, sad Hour selected from all years
To mourn our loss, rouse thy obscure compeers,
And teach them thine own sorrow! Say: With me
Died Adonais! Till the future dares
Forget the past, his fate and fame shall be
An echo and a light unto eternity.

2

Where wert thou, mighty Mother, when he lay,
When thy Son lay, pierced by the shaft which flies
In darkness? where was lorn Urania
When Adonais died? With veilèd eyes,
'Mid listening Echoes, in her paradise
She sate, while one, with soft enamoured breath,
Rekindled all the fading melodies
With which, like flowers that mock the corse beneath,
He had adorned and hid the coming bulk of Death.

3

Oh weep for Adonais—he is dead!
Wake, melancholy Mother, wake and weep!

Yet wherefore? Quench within their burning bed
Thy fiery tears, and let thy loud heart keep,
Like his, a mute and uncomplaining sleep;
For he is gone where all things wise and fair
Descend. Oh dream not that the amorous deep
Will yet restore him to the vital air;
Death feeds on his mute voice, and ????? despair.

4
Most musical of mourners, weep again!
Lament anew, Urania!—He died
Who was the sire of an immortal strain,
Blind, old, and lonely, when his country's pride
The priest, the slave, and the liberticide,
Trampled and mocked with many a loathèd rite
Of lust and blood. He went unterrified
Into the gulf of death; but his clear Sprite
Yet reigns o'er earth, the third among the Sons of Light.

5
Most musical of mourners, weep anew!
Not all to that bright station dared to climb:
And happier they their happiness who knew,
Whose tapers yet burn through that night of time
In which suns perished. Others more sublime,
Struck by the envious wrath of man or God,
Have sunk, extinct in their refulgent prime;
And some yet live, treading the thorny road
Which leads, through toil and hate, to Fame's serene abode.

6
But now thy youngest, dearest one has perished,
The nursling of thy widowhood, who grew,

Like a pale flower by some sad maiden cherished,
And fed with true love tears instead of dew.
Most musical of mourners, weep anew!
Thy extreme hope, the loveliest and the last,
The bloom whose petals, nipt before they blew,
Died on the promise of the fruit, is waste;
The broken lily lies—the storm is overpast.

7

To that high Capital where kingly Death
Keeps his pale court in beauty and decay
He came; and bought, with price of purest breath,
A grave among the eternal.—Come away!
Haste, while the vault of blue Italian day
Is yet his fitting charnel-roof, while still
He lies as if in dewy sleep he lay.
Awake him not! surely he takes his fill
Of deep and liquid rest, forgetful of all ill.

8

He will awake no more, oh never more!
Within the twilight chamber spreads apace
The shadow of white Death, and at the door
Invisible Corruption waits to trace
His extreme way to her dim dwelling-place;
The eternal Hunger sits, but pity and awe
Soothe her pale rage, nor dares she to deface
So fair a prey, till darkness and the law
Of change shall o'er his sleep the mortal curtain draw.

9

Oh weep for Adonais!—The quick Dreams,
The passion-winged ministers of thought,

Who were his flocks, whom near the living streams
Of his young spirit he fed, and whom he taught
The love which was its music, wander not—
Wander no more from kindling brain to brain,
But droop there whence they sprung; and mourn their lot
Round the cold heart where, after their sweet pain,
They ne'er will gather strength or find a home again.

10

And one with trembling hands clasps his cold head,
And fans him with her moonlight wings, and cries,
'Our love, our hope, our sorrow, is not dead!
See, on the silken fringe of his faint eyes,
Like dew upon a sleeping flower, there lies
A tear some Dream has loosened from his brain.'
Lost Angel of a ruined Paradise!
She knew not 'twas her own,—as with no stain
She faded, like a cloud which had outwept its rain.

11

One from a lucid urn of starry dew
Washed his light limbs, as if embalming them;
Another clipt her profuse locks, and threw
The wreath upon him, like an anadem
Which frozen tears instead of pearls begem;
Another in her wilful grief would break
Her bow and wingèd reeds, as if to stem
A greater loss with one which was more weak,
And dull the barbèd fire against his frozen cheek.

12

Another Splendour on his mouth alit,
That mouth whence it was wont to draw the breath

Which gave it strength to pierce the guarded wit,
And pass into the panting heart beneath
With lightning and with music: the damp death
Quenched its caress upon his icy lips;
And, as a dying meteor stains a wreath
Of moonlight vapour which the cold night clips,
It flushed through his pale limbs, and passed to its eclipse.

13
And others came,—Desires and Adorations,
Wingèd Persuasions, and veiled Destinies,
Splendours, and Glooms, and glimmering Incarnations
Of Hopes and Fears, and twilight Phantasies;
And Sorrow, with her family of Sighs,
And Pleasure, blind with tears, led by the gleam
Of her own dying smile instead of eyes,
Came in slow pomp;—the moving pomp might seem
Like pageantry of mist on an autumnal stream.

14
All he had loved, and moulded into thought
From shape and hue and odour and sweet sound,
Lamented Adonais. Morning sought
Her eastern watch-tower, and her hair unbound,
Wet with the tears which should adorn the ground,
Dimmed the aerial eyes that kindle day;
Afar the melancholy Thunder moaned,
Pale Ocean in unquiet slumber lay,
And the wild Winds flew round, sobbing in their dismay.

15
Lost Echo sits amid the voiceless mountains,
And feeds her grief with his remembered lay,

And will no more reply to winds or fountains,
Or amorous birds perched on the young green spray,
Or herdsman's horn, or bell at closing day;
Since she can mimic not his lips, more dear
Than those for whose disdain she pined away
Into a shadow of all sounds:—a drear
Murmur, between their songs, is all the woodmen hear.

16
Grief made the young Spring wild, and she threw down
Her kindling buds, as if she Autumn were,
Or they dead leaves; since her delight is flown,
For whom should she have waked the sullen Year?
To Phoebus was not Hyacinth so dear,
Nor to himself Narcissus, as to both
Thou, Adonais; wan they stand and sere
Amid the faint companions of their youth,
With dew all turned to tears,—odour, to sighing ruth.

17
Thy spirit's sister, the lorn nightingale,
Mourns not her mate with such melodious pain;
Not so the eagle, who like thee could scale
Heaven, and could nourish in the sun's domain
Her mighty youth with morning, doth complain,
Soaring and screaming round her empty nest,
As Albion wails for thee: the curse of Cain
Light on his head who pierced thy innocent breast,
And scared the angel soul that was its earthly guest!

18
Ah woe is me! Winter is come and gone,
But grief returns with the revolving year.

The airs and streams renew their joyous tone;
The ants, the bees, the swallows, re-appear;
Fresh leaves and flowers deck the dead Seasons' bier;
The amorous birds now pair in every brake,
And build their mossy homes in field and brere;
And the green lizard and the golden snake,
Like unimprisoned flames, out of their trance awake.

19

Through wood and stream and field and hill and ocean,
A quickening life from the Earth's heart has burst,
As it has ever done, with change and motion,
From the great morning of the world when first
God dawned on chaos. In its steam immersed,
The lamps of heaven flash with a softer light;
All baser things pant with life's sacred thirst,
Diffuse themselves, and spend in love's delight
The beauty and the joy of their renewèd might.

20

The leprous corpse, touched by this spirit tender,
Exhales itself in flowers of gentle breath;
Like incarnations of the stars, when splendour
Is changed to fragrance, they illumine death,
And mock the merry worm that wakes beneath.
Nought we know dies: shall that alone which knows
Be as a sword consumed before the sheath
By sightless lightning? Th' intense atom glows
A moment, then is quenched in a most cold repose.

21

Alas that all we loved of him should be,
But for our grief, as if it had not been,

And grief itself be mortal! Woe is me!
Whence are we, and why are we? of what scene
The actors or spectators? Great and mean
Meet massed in death, who lends what life must borrow.
As long as skies are blue and fields are green,
Evening must usher night, night urge the morrow,
Month follow month with woe, and year wake year to sorrow.

22

He will awake no more, oh never more!
'Wake thou,' cried Misery, 'childless Mother, rise
Out of thy sleep, and slake in thy heart's core
A wound more fierce than his, with tears and sighs.'
And all the Dreams that watched Urania's eyes,
And all the Echoes whom their Sister's song
Had held in holy silence, cried 'Arise!'
Swift as a thought by the snake memory stung,
From her ambrosial rest the fading Splendour sprung.

She rose like an autumnal Night that springs
Out of the East, and follows wild and drear
The golden Day, which on eternal wings,
Even as a ghost abandoning a bier,
Had left the Earth a corpse. Sorrow and fear
So struck, so roused, so rapt Urania;
So saddened round her like an atmosphere
Of stormy mist; so swept her on her way,
Even to the mournful place where Adonais lay.

24

Out of her secret Paradise she sped,
Through camps and cities rough with stone and steel,
And human hearts, which, to her aery tread

Yielding not, wounded the invisible
Palms of her tender feet where'er they fell.
And barbèd tongues, and thoughts more sharp than they,
Rent the soft form they never could repel,
Whose sacred blood, like the young tears of May,
Paved with eternal flowers that undeserving way.

25
In the death-chamber for a moment Death,
Shamed by the presence of that living Might,
Blushed to annihilation, and the breath
Revisited those lips, and life's pale light
Flashed through those limbs, so late her dear delight.
'Leave me not wild and drear and comfortless,
As silent lightning leaves the starless night!
Leave me not!' cried Urania. Her distress
Roused Death: Death rose and smiled, and met her vain caress.

26
'Stay yet awhile! speak to me once again!
Kiss me, so long but as a kiss may live!
And in my heartless breast and burning brain
That word, that kiss, shall all thoughts else survive,
With food of saddest memory kept alive,
Now thou art dead, as if it were a part
Of thee, my Adonais! I would give
All that I am, to be as thou now art:—
But I am chained to Time, and cannot thence depart.

27
'O gentle child, beautiful as thou wert,
Why didst thou leave the trodden paths of men
Too soon, and with weak hands though mighty heart

Dare the unpastured dragon in his den?
Defenceless as thou wert, oh where was then
Wisdom the mirrored shield, or scorn the spear?—
Or, hadst thou waited the full cycle when
Thy spirit should have filled its crescent sphere,
The monsters of life's waste had fled from thee like deer.

28

'The herded wolves bold only to pursue,
The obscene ravens clamorous o'er the dead,
The vultures to the conqueror's banner true,
Who feed where Desolation first has fed,
And whose wings rain contagion,—how they fled,
When like Apollo, from his golden bow,
The Pythian of the age one arrow sped,
And smiled!—The spoilers tempt no second blow,
They fawn on the proud feet that spurn them lying low.

29

'The sun comes forth, and many reptiles spawn;
He sets, and each ephemeral insect then
Is gathered into death without a dawn,
And the immortal stars awake again.
So is it in the world of living men:
A godlike mind soars forth, in its delight
Making earth bare and veiling heaven; and, when
It sinks, the swarms that dimmed or shared its light
Leave to its kindred lamps the spirit's awful night.'

30

Thus ceased she: and the Mountain Shepherds came,
Their garlands sere, their magic mantles rent.
The Pilgrim of Eternity, whose fame

Over his living head like heaven is bent,
An early but enduring monument,
Came, veiling all the lightnings of his song
In sorrow. From her wilds Ierne sent
The sweetest lyrist of her saddest wrong,
And love taught grief to fall like music from his tongue.

31
'Midst others of less note came one frail Form,
A phantom among men, companionless
As the last cloud of an expiring storm
Whose thunder is its knell. He, as I guess,
Had gazed on Nature's naked loveliness
Actaeon-like; and now he fled astray
With feeble steps o'er the world's wilderness,
And his own thoughts along that rugged way
Pursued like raging hounds their father and their prey.

32
A pard-like Spirit beautiful and swift—
A love in desolation masked—a power
Girt round with weakness; it can scarce uplift
The weight of the superincumbent hour.
It is a dying lamp, a falling shower,
A breaking billow;—even whilst we speak
Is it not broken? On the withering flower
The killing sun smiles brightly: on a cheek
The life can burn in blood even while the heart may break.

33
His head was bound with pansies overblown,
And faded violets, white and pied and blue;
And a light spear topped with a cypress cone,

Round whose rude shaft dark ivy tresses grew
Yet dripping with the forest's noonday dew,
Vibrated, as the ever-beating heart
Shook the weak hand that grasped it. Of that crew
He came the last, neglected and apart;
A herd-abandoned deer struck by the hunter's dart.

34

All stood aloof, and at his partial moan
Smiled through their tears; well knew that gentle band
Who in another's fate now wept his own;
As in the accents of an unknown land,
He sang new sorrow; sad Urania scanned
The Stranger's mien, and murmured 'Who art thou?'
He answered not, but with a sudden hand
Made bare his branded and ensanguined brow,
Which was like Cain's or Christ's—Oh that it should be so!

35

What softer voice is hushed over the dead?
Athwart what brow is that dark mantle thrown?
What form leans sadly o'er the white death-bed,
In mockery of monumental stone,
The heavy heart heaving without a moan?
If it be he who, gentlest of the wise,
Taught, soothed, loved, honoured, the departed one,
Let me not vex with inharmonious sighs
The silence of that heart's accepted sacrifice.

36

Our Adonais has drunk poison—oh
What deaf and viperous murderer could crown
Life's early cup with such a draught of woe?

The nameless worm would now itself disown;
It felt, yet could escape, the magic tone
Whose prelude held all envy, hate, and wrong,
But what was howling in one breast alone,
Silent with expectation of the song
Whose master's hand is cold, whose silver lyre unstrung.

37

Live thou, whose infamy is not thy fame!
Live! fear no heavier chastisement from me,
Thou noteless blot on a remembered name!
But be thyself, and know thyself to be!
And ever at thy season be thou free
To spill the venom when thy fangs o'erflow:
Remorse and self-contempt shall cling to thee,
Hot shame shall burn upon thy secret brow,
And like a beaten hound tremble thou shalt—as now.

38

Nor let us weep that our delight is fled
Far from these carrion kites that scream below.
He wakes or sleeps with the enduring dead;
Thou canst not soar where he is sitting now.—
Dust to the dust: but the pure spirit shall flow
Back to the burning fountain whence it came,
A portion of the Eternal, which must glow
Through time and change unquenchably the same,
Whilst thy cold embers choke the sordid hearth of shame.

39

Peace, peace! he is not dead, he doth not sleep—
He hath awakened from the dream of life.
'Tis we who, lost in stormy visions, keep

With phantoms an unprofitable strife,
And in mad trance strike with our spirit's knife
Invulnerable nothings. *We* decay
Like corpses in a charnel; fear and grief
Convulse us and consume us day by day,
And cold hopes swarm like worms within our living clay.

40

He has outsoared the shadow of our night.
Envy and calumny and hate and pain,
And that unrest which men miscall delight,
Can touch him not and torture not again.
From the contagion of the world's slow stain
He is secure; and now can never mourn
A heart grown cold, a head grown grey in vain—
Nor, when the spirit's self has ceased to burn,
With sparkless ashes load an unlamented urn.

41

He lives, he wakes—'tis Death is dead, not he;
Mourn not for Adonais.—Thou young Dawn,
Turn all thy dew to splendour, for from thee
The spirit thou lamentest is not gone!
Ye caverns and ye forests, cease to moan!
Cease, ye faint flowers and fountains! and thou Air,
Which like a mourning veil thy scarf hadst thrown
O'er the abandoned Earth, now leave it bare
Even to the joyous stars which smile on its despair!

42

He is made one with Nature: there is heard
His voice in all her music, from the moan
Of thunder to the song of night's sweet bird.

He is a presence to be felt and known
In darkness and in light, from herb and stone,
Spreading itself where'er that Power may move
Which has withdrawn his being to its own,
Which wields the world with never wearied love,
Sustains it from beneath, and kindles it above.

43
He is a portion of the loveliness
Which once he made more lovely. He doth bear
His part, while the One Spirit's plastic stress
Sweeps through the dull dense world; compelling there
All new successions to the forms they wear;
Torturing th' unwilling dross, that checks its flight,
To its own likeness, as each mass may bear;
And bursting in its beauty and its might
From trees and beasts and men into the heaven's light.

44
The splendours of the firmament of time
May be eclipsed, but are extinguished not;
Like stars to their appointed height they climb,
And death is a low mist which cannot blot
The brightness it may veil. When lofty thought
Lifts a young heart above its mortal lair,
And love and life contend in it for what
Shall be its earthly doom, the dead live there,
And move like winds of light on dark and stormy air.

45
The inheritors of unfulfilled renown
Rose from their thrones, built beyond mortal thought,
Far in the unapparent. Chatterton

Rose pale, his solemn agony had not
Yet faded from him; Sidney, as he fought
And as he fell and as he lived and loved
Sublimely mild, a spirit without spot,
Arose; and Lucan, by his death approved:
Oblivion as they rose shrank like a thing reproved.

46

And many more, whose names on earth are dark,
But whose transmitted effluence cannot die
So long as fire outlives the parent spark,
Rose, robed in dazzling immortality.
'Thou art become as one of us,' they cry;
'It was for thee yon kingless sphere has long
Swung blind in unascended majesty,
Silent alone amid an heaven of song.
Assume thy wingèd throne, thou Vesper of our throng!'

47

Who mourns for Adonais? Oh come forth,
Fond wretch, and know thyself and him aright.
Clasp with thy panting soul the pendulous earth;
As from a centre, dart thy spirit's light
Beyond all worlds, until its spacious might
Satiate the void circumference: then shrink
Even to a point within our day and night;
And keep thy heart light lest it make thee sink
When hope has kindled hope, and lured thee to the brink.

48

Or go to Rome, which is the sepulchre,
Oh not of him, but of our joy. 'Tis nought
That ages, empires, and religions, there

Lie buried in the ravage they have wrought;
For such as he can lend—they borrow not
Glory from those who made the world their prey;
And he is gathered to the kings of thought
Who waged contention with their time's decay,
And of the past are all that cannot pass away.

49

Go thou to Rome,—at once the paradise,
The grave, the city, and the wilderness;
And where its wrecks like shattered mountains rise,
And flowering weeds and fragrant copses dress
The bones of Desolation's nakedness,
Pass, till the Spirit of the spot shall lead
Thy footsteps to a slope of green access,
Where, like an infant's smile, over the dead
A light of laughing flowers along the grass is spread.

50

And grey walls moulder round, on which dull Time
Feeds, like slow fire upon a hoary brand;
And one keen pyramid with wedge sublime,
Pavilioning the dust of him who planned
This refuge for his memory, doth stand
Like flame transformed to marble; and beneath
A field is spread, on which a newer band
Have pitched in heaven's smile their camp of death,
Welcoming him we lose with scarce extinguished breath.

51

Here pause. These graves are all too young as yet
To have outgrown the sorrow which consigned
Its charge to each; and, if the seal is set

Here on one fountain of a mourning mind,
Break it not thou! too surely shalt thou find
Thine own well full, if thou returnest home,
Of tears and gall. From the world's bitter wind
Seek shelter in the shadow of the tomb.
What Adonais is why fear we to become?

52

The One remains, the many change and pass;
Heaven's light for ever shines, earth's shadows fly;
Life, like a dome of many-coloured glass,
Stains the white radiance of eternity,
Until Death tramples it to fragments.—Die,
If thou wouldst be with that which thou dost seek!
Follow where all is fled!—Rome's azure sky,
Flowers, ruins, statues, music, words, are weak
The glory they transfuse with fitting truth to speak.

53

Why linger, why turn back, why shrink, my heart?
Thy hopes are gone before: from all things here
They have departed; thou shouldst now depart!
A light is past from the revolving year,
And man and woman; and what still is dear
Attracts to crush, repels to make thee wither.
The soft sky smiles, the low wind whispers near:
'Tis Adonais calls! Oh hasten thither!
No more let Life divide what Death can join together.

54

That light whose smile kindles the universe,
That beauty in which all things work and move,
That benediction which the eclipsing curse

Of birth can quench not, that sustaining Love
Which, through the web of being blindly wove
By man and beast and earth and air and sea,
Burns bright or dim, as each are mirrors of
The fire for which all thirst, now beams on me,
Consuming the last clouds of cold mortality.

55

The breath whose might I have invoked in song
Descends on me; my spirit's bark is driven
Far from the shore, far from the trembling throng
Whose sails were never to the tempest given.
The massy earth and spherèd skies are riven!
I am borne darkly, fearfully, afar;
Whilst, burning through the inmost veil of heaven,
The soul of Adonais, like a star,
Beacons from the abode where the Eternal are.

CANCELLED PASSAGES OF ADONAIS, AND OF ITS PREFACE

THE expression of my indignation and sympathy. I will allow myself a first and last word on the subject of calumny as it relates to me. As an author I have dared and invited censure. If I understand myself, I have written neither for profit nor for fame: I have employed my poetical compositions and publications simply as the instruments of that sympathy between myself and others which the ardent and un-bounded love I cherished for my kind incited me to acquire. I expected all sorts of stupidity and insolent contempt from those. . . . These compositions (excepting the tragedy of *The Cenci,* which was written rather to try my powers than to unbur-den my full heart) are insufficiently. . . . Commendation then perhaps they deserve, even from their bitterest enemies; but they have not obtained any corresponding popularity. As a man, I shrink from notice and regard; the ebb and flow of the world vexes me: I desire to be left in peace. Persecution, contumely, and calumny, have been heaped upon me in profuse measure; and domestic conspiracy and legal oppression have violated in my person the most sacred rights of nature and humanity. The bigot will say it was the recompense of my errors—the man of the world will call it the result of my imprudence; but never as upon one head. . . .

Reviewers, with some rare exceptions, are a most stupid and malignant race. As a bankrupt thief turns thief-taker in despair, so an unsuccessful author turns critic. But a young spirit panting for fame, doubtful of its powers, and certain only of its aspirations, is ill-qualified to assign its true value to the sneer of this world. He knows not that such stuff as this is of the abortive and monstrous births which time consumes as fast as it produces. He sees the truth and falsehood, the merits and demerits, of his case, inextricably entangled. . . . No personal offence should have drawn from me this public comment upon such stuff.

The offence of this poor victim seems to have consisted solely in his intimacy with Leigh Hunt, Mr. Hazlitt, and some other enemies of despotism and superstition. My friend Hunt has a very hard skull to crack, and will take a deal of killing. I do not know much of Mr. Hazlitt, but. . .

I knew personally but little of Keats; but, on the news of his situation, I wrote to him, suggesting the propriety of trying the Italian climate, and inviting him to join me. Unfortunately he did not allow me

1
AND the green paradise which western waves
Embosom in their ever-wailing sweep,—
Talking of freedom to their tongueless caves,
Or to the spirits which within them keep
A record of the wrongs which, though they sleep,
Die not, but dream of retribution,—heard
His hymns, and echoing them from steep to steep,
Kept—......

2

And ever as he went he swept a lyre
Of unaccustomed shape, and . . . strings
Now like the . . . of impetuous fire
Which shakes the forest with its murmurings,
Now like the rush of the aerial wings
Of the enamoured wind among the treen,
Whispering unimaginable things,
And dying on the streams of dew serene
Which feed the unmown meads with ever-during green......

3

And then came one of sweet and earnest looks,
Whose soft smiles to his dark and night-like eyes
Were as the clear and ever-living brooks
Are to the obscure fountains whence they rise,
Showing how pure they are: a paradise
Of happy truth upon his forehead low
Lay, making wisdom lovely, in the guise
Of earth-awakening morn upon the brow
Of star-deserted heaven while ocean gleams below.

4

His song, though very sweet, was low and faint,
A simple strain.
......

5

A mighty Phantasm, half concealed
In darkness of his own exceeding light,
Which clothed his awful presence unrevealed,
Charioted on the...night

Of thunder-smoke, whose skirts were chrysolite.

6
And like a sudden meteor which outstrips
The splendour-winged chariot of the sun,
.......eclipse
The armies of the golden stars, each one
Pavilioned in its tent of light—all strewn
Over the chasms of blue night——

NOTES

TITLE AND PREFACE

Line 1. ***Adonais.*** There is nothing to show positively why Shelley adopted the name Adonais as a suitable Hellenic name for John Keats. I have already suggested (p. 62) that he may perhaps have wished to indicate, in this indirect way, that his poem was founded partly upon the Elegy of Bion for Adonis. I believe the name Adonais was not really in use among the Greeks, and is not anywhere traceable in classical Grecian literature. It has sometimes been regarded as a Doricized form of the name Adonis: Mr. William Cory says that it is not this, but would properly be a female form of the same name. Dr. Furnivall has suggested to me that Adonais is 'Shelley's variant of Adonias, the women's yearly mourning for Adonis.' Disregarding details, we may perhaps say that the whole subject of his Elegy is treated by Shelley as a transposition of the lament, as conceived by Bion, of the Cyprian Aphrodite for Adonis; and that, as he changes the Cyprian into the Uranian Aphrodite, so he changes the dead youth from Adonis into Adonais. 'Adonais' might possibly mean 'a poem about Adonis,' 'a lament for Adonis' (cp. such words as Thebais, &c.). But (to revert to the use of Adonais as a personal name) the melody of the syllables, possibly also some recollection of the Hebrew Adonai, may have led Shelley to use it in place of 'Adonis.' So Keats of Endymion,

'The very music of the name has gone
Into my being.'

The ideal beauty of Adonis and his early death made him a suitable poetical counterpart to Keats. Besides Bion's Elegy the beautiful hymn introduced into the fifteenth Idyll of Theocritus (a favourite poet of Shelley's) should be remembered.

1. 4. ***Motto from the poet Plato.*** This motto has been translated by Shelley himself as follows:

'Thou wert the morning star among the living,
Ere thy fair light had fled:—
Now, having died, thou art as Hesperus, giving
New splendour to the dead.'

1. 3. ***Motto from Moschus.*** Translated on p. 70, 'Poison came, Bion,' &c.

1. 13. ***It is my intention to subjoin to the London edition of this poem a criticism,*** &c. As to the non-fulfilment of this intention see p. 32.

1. 16. ***My known repugnance . . . proves at least.*** In the Pisa edition the word is printed 'prove' (not 'proves'). Shelley was far from being an exact writer in matters of this sort. Cp. the letter written (but not sent) to the editor of the ***Quarterly Review*** :—'I speak impartially, for the canons of taste to which Keats has conformed in his other (i. e. other than ***Hyperion***) compositions are the very reverse of my own.'

1. 22. ***John Keats died . . . in his twenty-fourth year, on the*** [23rd] ***of*** [***February***] 1821. Keats, at the time of his death, was not really in his twenty-fourth, but in his twenty-sixth year: the date of his birth was October 31, 1795. In the Pisa edition of ***Adonais*** the date of death is given thus—'the—of—1821': for Shelley, when he wrote his Preface, had no precise knowledge of the facts. In some later edi-

tions, 'the 27th of December 1820' was erroneously substituted. Shelley's mistake in supposing that Keats, in 1821, was aged only twenty-three, may be taken into account in estimating his previous observation, 'I consider the fragment of *Hyperion* as second to nothing that was ever produced by a writer of the same years.' Keats, writing in August 1820, had told Shelley (see p. 17) that some of his poems, perhaps including *Hyperion,* had been written 'above two years' preceding that date. If Shelley supposed that Keats was twenty-three years old at the beginning of 1821, and that *Hyperion* had been written fully two years prior to August 1820, he must have accounted that poem to be the product of a youth of twenty, or at most twenty-one, which would indeed be a marvellous instance of precocity. As a matter of fact, *Hyperion* was written by Keats when in his twenty-fourth year. This diminishes the marvel, but does not make Shelley's comment on the poem any the less correct.

1. 24. *Was buried in the romantic and lonely cemetery of the Protestants in that city, under the pyramid which is the tomb of Cestius.* As to the burial of the ashes of Shelley himself in a separate portion of the same cemetery, see p. 24. Cp. letter written from Rome in December 1818, quoted in the note on stanza 49, 1. 7. See also on stanzas 50 and 51.

1. 36. *The savage criticism on his* Endymion *which appeared in the* Quarterly Review. As to this matter see the prefatory Memoirs of Shelley and of Keats, and especially, at p. 41, &c., a transcript of the criticism.

1. 39. *The agitation thus originated ended in the rupture of a blood-vessel in the lungs.* See pp. 28 and 39. The *Quarterly* critique was published in September 1818, and the first rupture of a blood-vessel occurred in February 1820. Whether the mortification felt by Keats at the critique was small (as is now generally opined) or great (as Shelley thought), it cannot reasonably be propounded that this caused, or resulted in, the rupture of the pulmonary blood-vessel. Keats belonged to a consumptive family; his mother died of consumption, and also his younger brother: and the preliminaries of his mortal illness (even if we do not date them farther back,

for which some reason appears) began towards the middle of July 1818, when, in very rough walking in the Island of Mull, he caught a severe and persistent attack of sore throat.

1. 41. *The succeeding acknowledgments, from more candid critics, of the true greatness of his powers.* The notice here principally referred to is probably that which appeared in the *Edinburgh Review* in August 1820, written by Lord Jeffrey.

1. 46. *Whether the poisoned shaft lights on a heart made callous by many blows.* Shelley, in this expression, has no doubt himself in view. He had had serious reason for complaining of the treatment meted out to him by the *Quarterly Review* : see the opening (partially cited at p. 18) of his draft-letter to the Editor.

1. 48. *One of their associates is, to my knowledge, a most base and unprincipled calumniator.* Shelley here refers to the writer of the critique in the *Quarterly Review* of his poem *Laon and Cythna* (*The Revolt of Islam*). At first he supposed the writer to be Southey; afterwards, the Rev. H. H. (Dean) Milman. His Indignant phrase is therefore levelled at Milman. But Shelley was mistaken, for the article was in fact written by Mr. (afterwards Judge) Coleridge.

1. 51. *Those who had celebrated with various degrees of complacency and panegyric Paris, and* Woman, *and* A Syrian Tale, *and Mrs. Lefanu, and Mr. Barrett, and Mr. Howard Payne.* I presume that most readers of the present day are in the same position as I was myself—that of knowing nothing about these performances and their authors. In order to understand Shelley's allusion, I looked up the *Quarterly Review* from April 1817 to April 1821, and have ascertained as follows. (1) The *Quarterly* of April 1817 contains a notice of *Paris in 1815, a Poem.* The author was the Rev. George Croly, but the title-page does not give his name. The poem, numbering about a thousand lines, is in the Spenserian stanza, varied by the heroic metre, and perhaps by some other rhythms. Numerous extracts are given, sufficient to show that the poem is at any rate a creditable piece of writing.

Some of the critical dicta are the following:—'The work of a powerful and poetic imagination. . . . The subject of the poem is a desultory walk through Paris, in which the author observes, with very little regularity but with great force, on the different objects which present themselves. . . . Sketching with the hand of a master. . . . In a strain of poetry and pathos which we have seldom seen equalled. . . . An admirable poet.' (2) ***Woman*** is a poem by the Mr. Barrett whom Shelley names, termed on the title-page 'the Author of ***The Heroine.*** ' It was noticed in the ***Quarterly*** for April 1818, the very same number which contained the sneering critique of ***Endymion***. This poem is written in the heroic metre; and the extracts given do certainly comprise some telling and felicitous lines. Such are:—

'The beautiful rebuke that looks surprise,
The gentle vengeance of averted eyes;'

also (a line which has borne, and may yet bear, frequent requoting)

'Last at his cross, and earliest at his grave.'

For critical utterances we have the ensuing:—'A strain of patriotism pure, ardent, and even sublime. . . . Versification combining conciseness and strength with a considerable degree of harmony. . . . Both talent and genius. . . . Some passages of it, and those not a few, are of the first order of the pathetic and descriptive.' (3) ***A Syrian Tale.*** Of this book I have failed to find any trace in the ***Quarterly Review***, or in the Catalogue of the British Museum. (4) Mrs. Lefanu. Neither can I trace this lady in the ***Quarterly***. Mrs. Alicia Lefanu, who is stated to have been a sister of Richard Brinsley Sheridan, and also her daughter, Miss Alicia Lefanu, published books during the lifetime of Shelley. The former printed ***The Flowers, a Fairy Tale,*** 1810, and ***The Sons of Erin, a Comedy,*** 1812. To the latter various works are assigned, such as ***Rosara's Chain, a Poem.*** (5) Mr. John Howard Payne was author of ***Brutus, or the Fall of Tarquin, an Historical Tragedy,*** criticized in the ***Quarterly*** for April 1820. I cannot understand why Shelley should have supposed this criticism to be laudatory: it is in fact unmixed censure. As thus:—'He Appears to us to have no one quality which we should require in a tragic poet. . . . We cannot find in the whole play a single character finely conceived or rightly sustained, a single incident well managed, a single speech—nay a single sentence—of good poetry.' It is true that the same article which reviews Payne's **Brutus** notices also, and with more indulgence, Sheil's **Evadne** : possibly Shelley glanced at the article very cursorily, and fancied that any eulogistic phrases which he found in it applied to Payne.

1. 57. *A parallel between the Rev. Mr. Milman and Lord Byron.* I have not succeeded in finding this parallel. The **Quarterly Review** for July 1818 contains a critique of Milman's poem, **Samor, Lord of the Bright City;** and the number for May 1820, a critique of Milman's **Fall of Jerusalem.** Neither of these notices draws any parallel such as Shelley speaks of.

1. 58. *What gnat did they strain at here.* The word 'here' will be perceived to mean 'in **Endymion,** ' or 'in reference to **Endymion** '; but it is rather far separated from its right antecedent.

1. 66. *The circumstances of the closing scene of poor Keats's life were not made known to me until the Elegy was ready for the press.* See p. 23.

1. 71. *The poor fellow seems to have been hooted fro the stage of life, no less by those on whom he has wasted the promise of his genius than those on whom he had lavished his fortune and his care.* This statement of Shelley is certainly founded upon a passage in the letter (see p. 23) addressed by Colonel Finch to Mr. Gisborne. Colonel Finch said that Keats had reached Italy, 'nursing a deeply rooted disgust to life and to the world, owing to having been infamously treated by the very persons whom his generosity had rescued from want and woe.' The Colonel's statement seems (as I have previously intimated) to be rather haphazard; and Shelley's recast of it goes to a further extreme.

1. 77. '*Almost risked his own life,* ' &c. The substance of the words in inverted commas is contained in Colonel Finch's letter, but Shelley does not cite verbatim.

Stanza 1, 1. 1. I weep for Adonais—he is dead. Modelled on the opening of Bion's Elegy for Adonis. See p. 67.

11. 4, 5. *And thou, sad Hour, . . . rouse thy obscure compeers.* The compeers are clearly the other Hours. Why they should be termed 'obscure' is not quite manifest. Perhaps Shelley means that the weal or woe attaching to these Hours is obscure or uncertain; or perhaps that they are comparatively obscure, undistinguished, as not being marked by any such conspicuous event as the death of Adonais. For this appeal to the Hour of Adonais' death cp. *Hellas* :—

(Phantom loq.) 'Ask the cold pale Hour,
Rich in reversion of impending death,
When he shall fall. . . .'

Also the personification of the Hour (of Prometheus' release) in *Prometheus Unbound.* In the Adonis Hymn of Theocritus (Idyll xv. 104) the Hours bring back Adonis from Acheron:

11. 8, 9. *His fate and fame shall be An echo and a light unto eternity.* By 'eternity' we may here understand, not absolute eternity as contradistinguished from time, but an indefinite space of time, the years and the centuries. His fate and fame shall be echoed on from age to age, and shall be a light thereto. The Cambridge editors of 1829 considered that the lines 'Till the future dares . . . eternity' are not the speech of the Hour, but the poet's comment. Shelley's punctuation leaves this point open, and I regard it as rather uncertain.

Stanza 2, 1. 1. *Where wert thou, mighty Mother.* Aphrodite Urania. See pp. 51, 52. Shelley constantly uses the form 'wert' instead of 'wast.' This phrase may be modelled upon two lines near the opening of Milton's *Lycidas* :—

'Where were ye, nymphs, when the remorseless deep
Closed o'er the head of your loved Lycidas?'

which were suggested to Milton by Theocritus, i. 66:
cp. Virgil, Eclogue x. 9, 10.

11. 2, 3. *The shaft which flies In darkness.* As Adonis was mortally wounded by a boar's tusk, so (it is here represented) was Adonais slain by an insidiously or murderously launched dart: see p. 49. The allusion is to the attack made upon Keats by the *Quarterly Review.* It is true that 'the shaft which flies in darkness' might be understood in merely a general sense, as the mysterious and unforeseen arrow of Death: but I think it clear that Shelley used the phrase in a more special sense, and probably with an implied reference to *anonymous* criticism.

1. 4. With veilèd eyes, &c. Urania is represented as seated in her paradise (pleasure-ground, garden-bower), with veiled eyes—downward-lidded, as in slumber: an Echo chaunts or recites the 'melodies,' or poems, which Adonais had composed while Death was rapidly advancing towards him: Urania is surrounded by other Echoes, who hearken, and repeat the strain. The phrase, 'one with soft enamoured breath,' means 'one of the Echoes': this is shown in stanza 22, 'all the Echoes whom *their Sister's song,* ' &c.

Stanza 3, 11. 6, 7. *For he is gone where all things wise and fair Descend.* Founded on Bion (p. 68), 'Persephone, . . . all lovely things drift down to thee.'

1. 7. *The amorous deep.* The depth of earth, or region of the dead; amorous, because, having once obtained possession of Adonais, it retains him in a close embrace, and will not restore him to the land of the living. This passage has a certain analogy to that of Bion (p. 69), 'Not that he is loth to hear, but that the Maiden of Hades will not let him go.' Cp. *Romeo and Juliet,* Act v. sc. 3:—

'Shall I believe
That unsubstantial Death is amorous,
And that the lean abhorred monster keeps
Thee here in dark to be his paramour?'

Stanza 4, 1. 1. ***Most musical of mourners.*** This phrase is modelled upon Moschus iii. 71, &c.:—

This, O most musical of rivers, is thy new woe. Of old didst thou lose Homer . . . Now again another son thou weepest.

1. 2. ***He died.*** Milton.

1. 4. ***When his country's pride,*** &c. Construe: When the priest, the slave, and the liberticide, trampled his country's pride, and mocked [it] with many a loathed rite of lust and blood. This of course refers to the condition of public affairs and of court-life in the reign of Charles II. The inversion in this passage is not a very serious one, although, for the sense, slightly embarrassing. Occasionally Shelley conceded to himself great latitude in inversion: as for instance in the ***Revolt of Islam,*** canto 3, st. 34,

'And the swift boat the little waves which bore
Were cut by its keen keel, though slantingly,'

which means 'And the little waves, which bore the swift boat, were cut,' &c.; also in the ***Ode to Naples,*** strophe 4,

'Florence, beneath the sun,
Of cities fairest one,
Blushes within her bower for Freedom's expectation.'

1. 8. ***His clear Sprite.*** Shelley, who is exceedingly fond of the word 'Spirit,' uses the form Sprite in the ***Lines written among the Euganean Hills*** :—

'Every Sprite beneath the moon
Would repent its envy vain
And the earth grow young again.'

In our older poets, especially Spenser, this form is frequently used, even in the most sacred associations. Thus **Faery Queen,** v. 3. 40, 'To gather fresher Sprights,' and **Hymn of Heavenly Beautie,** stanza 2, 1. 1,

'Vouchsafe then, O thou most Almightie Spright.'

I question however, whether, according to the diction of Shelley's day, the term 'sprite' could reasonably be applied to Milton: I certainly think it could not at the present time.

1. 9. ***The third among the Sons of Light.*** At first sight this phrase might seem to mean 'the third-greatest poet of the world': in which case one might suppose Homer and Shakespeare to be ranked as the first and second. But it may be regarded as tolerably clear that Shelley is here thinking only of **epic** poets; and that he ranges the epic poets according to a criterion of his own, which is thus expressed in his **Defence of Poetry** (written in the same year as **Adonais,** 1821): 'Homer was the first and Dante the second epic poet; that is, the second poet the series of whose creations bore a defined and intelligible relation to the knowledge and sentiment and religion of the age in which he lived, and of the ages which followed it—developing itself in correspondence with their development. . . Milton was the third epic poet.' The poets whom Shelley admired most were probably Homer, Aeschylus, Sophocles, Lucretius, Dante, Shakespeare, and Milton; he took high delight in the **Book of Job,** and presumably in some other poetical books of the Old Testament; Calderon also he prized greatly; and in his own time Goethe, Byron, and (on some grounds) Wordsworth and Coleridge.

Stanza 5, 1. 2. ***Not all to that bright station dared to climb.*** The conception embodied in the diction of this stanza is not quite so clear as might be wished. The first statement seems to amount to this—That some poets, true poets though they were, did not aspire so high, nor were capable of reaching so high, as Homer, Dante, and Milton, the typical epic poets. A statement so obviously true that it hardly extends, in itself, beyond a truism. But it must be read as introductory to what follows.

1. 3. ***And happier they their happiness who knew.*** Clearly a recast of the phrase of Virgil,

'O fortunati nimium sua si bona norint
Agricolae.'

But Virgil speaks of men who did not adequately appreciate their own happiness; Shelley (apparently) of others who did so. He seems to intimate that the poetical temperament is a happy one, in the case of those poets who, unconcerned with the greatest ideas and the most arduous schemes of work, pour forth their 'native wood-notes wild.' I think it possible however that Shelley intended his phrase to be accepted with the same meaning as Virgil's—'happier they, supposing they had known their happiness.' In that case, the only reason implied why these minor poets were the happier is that their works have endured the longer.

11. 4, 5. ***Whose tapers yet burn through that night of time In which suns perished.*** Shelley here appears to say that the minor poets have left works which survive, while some of the works of the very greatest poets have disappeared: as, for instance, his own lyrical models in ***Adonais,*** Bion and Moschus, are still known by their writings, while many of the masterpieces of Aeschylus and Sophocles are lost. Buffon, whose ***Histoire Naturelle*** was published at Paris in 1749 and following years, writes in the chapter of vol. i. entitled 'Théorie de la Terre,' answering objections to the hypothesis that the planets were struck out of our sun by collision with a comet:—'D'ailleurs ne peut-on pas soupçonner que si le soleil ou une étoile brulante et lumineuse par elle-meme se mouvoit avec autant de vitesse que se meuvent les planètes, le feu s'éteindroit peut-etre, et que c'est par cette raison que toutes les étoiles que l'on appelle nouvelles, qui ont probablement changé de lieu, se sont éteintes aux yeux meme des observateurs. On pourroit répondre encore que le feu ne peut pas subsister aussi longtemps dans les petites que dans les grandes masses, et qu'au sortir du soleil les planètes ont du bruler quelque temps, mais qu'elles se sont éteintes faute de matières combustibles, comme le soleil s'éteindra probablement

par la meme raison, mais dans les ages futurs. ' (The italics are not Buffon's.) Buffon's *Theorie de la Terre* was one of the books read by the Shelleys in 1817. Its fascination appears earlier, in a letter written by the poet from Geneva in July 1816:—
'I will not pursue Buffon's sublime but gloomy theory—that the globe which we inhabit will, at some future period, be changed into a mass of frost by the encroachment of the polar ice.' Shelley's passionate interest in the phenomena of Nature, which was developed at Eton, but which dates from earlier years, supplies him with much of his poetical imagery, and gives it reality and precision.—Great luminaries (whether great poets, who, for whatever reason, have failed to realize their genius, or the works of such men) have been extinguished, while the taper light of lesser men and works has continued to shine. See also on stanza 44, 1. 1.

11. 5–7. *Others more sublime, Struck by the envious wrath of man or God, Have sunk, extinct in their refulgent prime.* These others include Keats (Adonais) himself, to whom the phrase, 'struck by the envious wrath of man,' may be understood as more peculiarly appropriated. And generally the 'others' may be regarded as nearly identical with 'the inheritors of unfulfilled renown' who appear (some of them pointed out by name) in stanza 45. The idea of envy on the part of the Gods against mortals who dared to vie with them is familiar in Greek mythology, illustrated by the fate of Niobe, Marsyas, and Thamyris.

11. 8, 9. *And some yet live, treading the thorny road Which leads, through toil and hate, to Fame's serene abode.* Byron must be supposed to be the foremost among these; also Wordsworth and Coleridge; and doubtless Shelley himself should not be omitted.

Stanza 6, 1. 2. *The nursling of thy widowhood.* As to this expression see p. 53. I was there speaking only of the Muse Urania; but the observations are equally applicable to Aphrodite Urania, and I am unable to carry the argument any further.

11. 3, 4. Like a pale flower by some sad maiden cherished, And fed with .

Stanzas 7-14. In the stanzas describing the vigil kept over the dead Adonais a progression of time is indicated by successive epithets and phrases:—blue Italian day—the twilight chamber—her moonlight "'wings—starry dew—the image at the end of stanza 12—Morning sought her eastern watch-tower.

Stanza 7, 1. 1. ***To that high Capital where kingly Death,*** &c. The Capital is Rome (where Keats died). Death is figured as the King of Rome, who there 'keeps his pale court in beauty and decay,'—amid the beauties of nature and art, and amid the decay of monuments and institutions.

11. 3, 4. ***And bought, with price of purest breath, A grave among the eternal.*** Keats, dying in Rome, secured sepulture among the many illustrious persons who are there buried. This seems to be the only meaning of 'the eternal' in the present passage: the term does not directly imply (what is sufficiently enforced elsewhere) Keat's own poetic immortality.

1. 4. ***Come away!*** This call is addressed in fancy to any persons present in the chamber of death. They remain indefinite both to the poet and to the reader. They conclusion of the stanza, worded with great beauty and delicacy, amounts substantially to saying—'Take your last look of the dead Adonais while he may still seem to the eye to be rather sleeping than dead.'

1. 7. ***He lies as if in dewy sleep he lay.*** See Bion (p. 68), 'Beautiful in death, as on that hath fallen on sleep.' The term 'dewy sleep' means probably 'sleep which refreshes the body as nightly dew refreshes the fields.' This phrase is followed by the kindred expression 'liquid rest.'

Stanza 8, 1. 3. ***The shadow of white Death,*** &c. The use of 'his' and 'her' in this stanza is not wholly free from ambiguity. In st. 7 Death was a male impersonation—'kingly Death' who 'keeps his pale court.' It may be assumed that he is the same in the present stanza. Corruption, on the other hand, is a female impersonation: she (not Death) must be the same as 'the eternal Hunger,' as to whom it is said that 'pity and awe soothe ***her*** pale rage.' Premising this, we read:—'Within the twilight chamber spreads apace the shadow of white Death, and at the door invisible

Corruption waits to trace his [Adonais's] extreme way to her [Corruption's] dim dwelling-place; the eternal Hunger [Corruption] sits [at the door], but pity and awe soothe her pale rage, nor dares she,' &c. The unwonted phrase 'his extreme way' seems to differ in meaning little if at all from the very ordinary term 'his last journey.' The statement in this stanza therefore is that corruption does not assail Adonais lying on his deathbed; but will shortly follow his remains to the grave, the dim [obscure, lightless] abode of corruption itself.

1. 6. With 'The eternal Hunger' cp. the lines in *A Vision of the Sea* (1820):—

'Like a corpse on the clay which is hung'ring to fold
Its corruption around it.'

11. 8, 9. *Till darkness and the law Of change shall o'er his sleep the mortal curtain draw.* Until the darkness of the grave and the universal law of change and dissolution shall draw the curtain of death over his sleep—shall prove his apparent sleep to be veritable death. The prolonged interchange in *Adonais* between the ideas of death and of sleep may remind us that Shelley opened with a similar contrast or approximation his first considerable (though in part immature) poem, *Queen Mab* :—

'How wonderful is Death,—
Death, and his brother Sleep!' &c.

The mind may also revert to the noble passage in Byron's *Giaour* :—

'He who hath bent him o'er the dead
Ere the first day of death is fled,' &c.—

though the idea of actual sleep is not raised in this admirably beautiful and admirably realistic description. Perhaps the poem, of all others, in which the conception of death is associated with that of sleep with the most poignant pathos, is that of Edgar Poe entitled *For Annie* :—

'Thank Heaven, the crisis,
The danger, is past,
And the lingering illness
Is over at last,
And the fever called living
Is conquered at last,' &c.—

where real death is spoken of throughout, in a series of exquisite and thrilling images, as being real sleep. In Shelley's own edition of *Adonais,* the lines which we are now considering are essentially different. They run

'Till darkness and the law
Of mortal change shall fill the grave which is her maw.'

This is comparatively poor and rude. The change to the present reading was introduced by Mrs. Shelley in her edition of Shelley's Poems in 1839. She gives no information as to her authority: but there can be no doubt that at some time or other Shelley himself made the improvement. See pp. 34, 35 and notes on 16, 28.

Stanza 9, 1. 1. *The quick Dreams.* With these words begins a passage of some length, which is closely modelled upon the passage of Bion (p. 68), 'And around him the Loves are weeping,' &c.: modelled upon it, and also systematically transposed from it. The transposition goes on the same lines as that of Adonis into Adonais, and of the Cyprian into the Uranian Aphrodite; i.e. the personal or fleshly Loves are spiritualized into Dreams (musings, reveries, conceptions) and other faculties or emotions of the mind. It is to be observed, moreover, that the trance of Adonis attended by Cupids forms an incident in Keats's own poem of *Endymion,* Book II:—

'For on a silken couch of rosy pride,
In midst of all, there lay a sleeping youth
Of fondest beauty; fonder, in fair sooth,

Than sighs could fathom or contentment reach.

Hard by
Stood serene Cupids, watching silently..
One, kneeling to a lyre, touched the strings,
Muffling to death the pathos with his wings,
And ever and anon uprose to look
At the youth's slumber; while another took
A willow-bough, distilling odorous dew,
And shook it on his hair; another flew
In through the woven roof, and fluttering-wise
Rained violets upon his sleeping eyes.'

1. 2. The passion-wingèd ministers of thought. The 'Dreams' are here defined as being thoughts (or ministers of thought) winged with passion; not mere abstract cogitations, but thoughts warm with the heart's blood, emotional conceptions—such thoughts as subserve the purposes of poetry, and enter into its structure; in a word, poetic thoughts.

1. 3. *Who were his flocks,* &c. These Dreams were in fact the very thoughts of Adonais, as conveyed in his poems. He being dead, they cannot assume new forms of beauty in any future poems, and cannot be thus diffused from mind to mind, but they remain mourning round their deceased herdsman, or master. It is possible that this image of a flock and a herdsman is consequent upon the phrase in the Elegy of Moschus for Bion—'Bion the herdsman is dead' (p. 69). The metaphorical application of the verbs , (to 'herd') to thoughts and the like is not uncommon in Greek. Shelley may have has in mind Moschus ii. 5:—

1. 8. *After their sweet pain,* i.e. cp. *Prometheus Unbound,* ii. 2. 40, 'So sweet that joy is almost pain.' The 'bitter-sweet' () of love is classical: cp. Catullus lxviii. 17:—

'Non est dea nescia nostri,

Quae dulcem curis miscet amaritiem.'

Stanza 10, 1. 2. ***And fans him with her moonlight wings.*** See Bion (p. 69), 'and another, from behind him, with his wings is fanning Adonis.' The epithet 'moonlight' may indicate either delicacy of colour, or faint luminosity—rather the latter.

1. 7. ***Lost Angel of a ruined Paradise.*** The ruined Paradise is the mind, now torpid in death, of Adonais. The 'Dream' which has been speaking is a lost angel of this Paradise, in the sense of being a messenger or denizen of the mind of Adonais, incapacitated for exercising any further action: indeed, the Dream forthwith fades, and is for ever extinct. Shelley had probably read the ***Paradise and the Peri*** of 'the lyrist of Ierne' (Thomas Moore—see stanza 30); and there may perhaps in this passage be a kind reminiscence of the lines:—

'One morn a Peri at the gate
Of Eden stood disconsolate: . . .
She wept to think her recreant race
Should e'er have lost that glorious place. . . .
The glorious Angel who was keeping
The gates of light beheld her weeping. . . .
A tear-drop glistened
Within his eyelids.'

1. 8. ***With no stain.*** Leaving no trace behind. The rhyme has entailed the use of the word 'stain,' which is otherwise a little arbitrary in this connexion.

1. 9. ***She faded, like a cloud which had outwept its rain.*** A rain-cloud which has fully discharged its rain would no longer constitute a cloud—it would be dispersed and gone. The image is therefore a very exact one for the Dream which, having accomplished its function, now fades away. There appears to be a further parallel intended—between the Dream whose existence closes in a ***tear,*** and the rain-cloud which has discharged its ***rain*** : this is of less moment, and verges upon a conceit This passage in ***Adonais*** is not without some analogy to one in Keats's ***Endymion***

(quoted on p. 44):—

'Therein
A melancholy spirit well might win
Oblivion, and melt out his essence fine
Into the winds.'
Compare the last lines of *The Cloud* (1820),
'I change, but I cannot die,' &c.

Stanza 11, 11. 1, 2. ***One from a lucid urn of starry dew Washed his light limbs, as if embalming them.*** See the passage from Bion (p. 68), 'One in a golden vessel bears water, and another laves the wound.' The expression 'starry dew' is rather peculiar: the dew may originally have 'starred' the grass, but, when collected into an urn, it must have lost this property: perhaps we should rather understand, nocturnal dew upon which the stars had been shining. It is difficult to see how the act of washing the limbs could simulate the process of embalming.

1. 3. ***Another clipt her profuse locks.*** See Bion (p. 68), 'clipping their locks for Adonis.' 'Profuse' is here accented on the first syllable; although indeed the line can be read with the accent, as is usual, on the second syllable.

11. 3–5. ***And threw The wreath upon him, like an anadem Which frozen tears instead of pearls begem.*** The wreath is the lock of hair—perhaps a plait or curl, for otherwise the term wreath is rather wide of the mark. The idea that the tears shed by this Dream herself (or perhaps other Dreams) upon the lock are 'frozen,' and thus stand in lieu of pearls upon an anadem or circlet, seems strained, and indeed incongruous: one might wish it away. There is a juvenile poem by Shelley (1811) named *The Tear,* where a tear is termed 'The pure gem' and 'the dim ice-drop.' This notion, badly worded in the very boyish composition of 1811, is essentially the same which recurs in this stanza of *Adonais.*

11. 6, 7. Another in her wilful grief would break Her bow and wingèd reeds. Follows Bion closely—'And one upon his shafts, another on his bow, is treading'

(p. 68). This is perfectly appropriate for the Loves, or Cupids: not equally so for the Dreams, for it is not so apparent what concern they have with bows and arrows. These may however be 'winged thoughts' or 'winged words'—. Mr. Andrew Lang observes (Introduction to his Theocritus volume, p. xl), 'In one or other of the sixteen Pompeian pictures of Venus and Adonis, the Loves are breaking their bows and arrows for grief, as in the hymn of Bion.'

11. 7, 8. *As if to stem A greater loss with one which was more weak.* 'To stem a loss' is a very lax phrase—and more especially 'to stem a loss with another loss.' 'To stem a torrent—or, the current of a river,' is a well-known expression, indicating one sort of material force in opposition to another. Hence we come to the figurative expression, 'to stem the torrent of his grief,' &c. Shelley seems to have yielded to a certain analogy in the sentiment, and also to the convenience of a rhyme, and thus to have permitted himself a phrase which is neither English nor consistent with sense. Line 8 appears to me extremely feeble throughout.

1. 9. And dull the barbèd fire against his frozen cheek. The construction runs— 'Another would break, &c., and [would] dull, &c.' The term 'the barbèd fire' represents of course 'the winged reeds,' or arrows: actual reeds or arrows are now transmuted into flame-tipped arrows (conformable to the spiritual or immaterial quality of the Dreams): the fire is to be quenched against the frost of the death-cold cheek of Adonais. 'Frozen tears—frozen cheek': Shelley would scarcely, I apprehend, have allowed this.

11 5, 6. *The damp death Quenched its caress upon his icy lips.* This phrase is not very clear. I understand it to mean—The damps of death [upon the visage of Adonais] quenched the caress of the Splendour [or Dream] imprinted on his icy lips. It might however be contended that the term 'the damp death' is use as an energetic synonym for the 'Splendour' itself. In this case the sense of the whole passage may be amplified thus: The Splendour, in imprinting its caress upon the icy lips of Adonais, had its caress quenched by the cold, and was itself converted into dampness and deathliness: it was no longer a Iuminous Splendour, but a vaporous and clammy form of death. The assumption that 'the damp death' stands as a synonym for the

'Splendour' obtains some confirmation from the succeeding phrase about the '*dying meteor*'—for this certainly seems used as a smile for the 'Splendour.'

l. 7. ***And, as a dying meteor,*** &c. The dying meteor, in this simile, must represent the Splendour; the wreath of moonlight vapour stands for the pale limbs of Adonais; the cold night may in a general way symbolize the night of death.

l. 9. ***It flushed through his pale limbs, and passed to its eclipse.*** The Splendour flushed through the limbs of Adonais, and so became eclipsed,—faded into nothingness. This terminates the episode of the 'quick Dreams,' beginning with stanza 9.

Stanza 13, l. 1. And others came,—Desires and Adorations, &c. Here Shelley has direct recourse, no longer to the Elegy of Bion for Adonis, but to the Elegy of Moschus for Bion. As he had spiritualized the impersonations of Bion, so he now spiritualizes those of Moschus. The Sicilian lyrist gives us (see p. 69) Apollo, Satyrs, Priapi, Panes, and Fountain-fairies. Shelley gives us Desires, Adorations, Persuasions, Destinies, Splendours, Glooms, Hopes, Fears, Phantasies, Sorrow, Sighs, and Pleasure. All these 'lament Adonais' (stanza 14): they are such emotional or abstract beings as 'he had loved, and moulded into thought from shape and hue and odour and sweet sound.' The adjectival epithets are worth noting for their poetic felicity: wingèd Persuasions (again hinting at), veiled Destinies, glimmering Hopes and Fears, twilight Phantasies.

l. 6. ***And Pleasure, blind with tears,*** &c. The Rev. Stopford Brooke, in an eloquent lecture delivered to the Shelley Society in June 1889, dwelt at some length upon the singular mythopoeic gift of the poet. These two lines are an instance in point, of a very condensed kind. Pleasure, heart-struck at the death of Adonais, has abrogated her own nature, and has become blinded with tears: her eyes can therefore serve no longer to guide her steps. Her smile too is dying, but not yet dead: it emits a faint gleam which, in default of eyes, serves to distinguish the path. If one regards this as a mere image, it may be allowed to approach close to a conceit: but it suggests a series of incidents and figurative details which may rather count as a compendious myth.

1. 8. Came in slow pomp;—the moving pomp might seem. The repetition of the word 'pomp' gives a certain poverty to the sound of this line: it can hardly, I think, have been deliberately intended. In other respects this stanza is one of the most melodious in the poem. There is moreover a happy balance of initial consonants in this and the following line, which disappears if another monosyllable is substituted for the second 'pomp.'

Stanza 14, 11. 3, 4. *Morning sought Her eastern watch-tower, and her hair unbound,* &c. Whether Shelley wished the reader to attribute any distinct naturalistic meaning to the 'hair' of Morning is a question which may admit of some doubt. If he did so, the 'hair unbound' is probably to be regarded as streaks of rain-cloud: these cloudlets ought to fertilize the soil with their moisture: but, instead of that, they merely dim the eyes of Morning, and dull the beginnings of day. In this instance, and in many other instances ensuing, Shelley represents natural powers or natural objects—morning, echo, flowers, &c.—as suffering some interruption or decay of essence or function, in sympathy with the stroke which has cut short the life of Adonais. It need hardly be said that, in doing this, he only follows a host of predecessors. He follows, for example, his special models Bion and Moschus. They probably followed earlier models: but I have failed in attempting to trace how far back beyond them this scheme of symbolism may have extended: something of it can be found in Theocritus. The legend—doubtless a very ancient one—that the sisters of Phaeton wept amber for his fall belongs to the same order of ideas (as a learned friend suggests to me).

1. 8. *Pale Ocean.* As not only the real Keats, but also the figurative Adonais, died in Rome, the ocean cannot be a feature in the immediate scene: it lies in the not very remote distance, felt rather than visible to sight. Of course, too, Ocean (as well as Thunder and Winds) is personated in this passage: he is a cosmic deity, lying pale in unquiet slumber.

Stanza 15. 1. 1. *Lost Echo sits,* &c. Echo is introduced into both the Grecian elegies, that of Moschus as well as that of Bion. Bion (p. 68) simply says that 'Echo resounds, "Adonis dead!"' But Moschus (p. 69), whom Shelley substantially follows, sets forth that 'Echo in the rocks laments that thou [Bion] art silent, and no more she mimics thy voice'; also, 'Echo, among the reeds, doth still feed upon thy songs.' It will be observed that in this stanza Echo is a single personage—the Nymph known to mythological fable: but in stanza 2 we had various 'Echoes,' spirits of minor account, who, in the paradise of Urania, were occupied with the poems of Adonais.

11. 6–8. *His lips, more dear Than those for whose disdain she pined away Into a shadow of all sounds.* Echo is, in mythology, a Nymph who was in love with Narcissus. He, being enamoured of his own beautiful countenance, paid no heed to Echo, who consequently 'pined away into a shadow of all sounds.' In this expression one may discern a delicate double meaning. (1) Echo pined away into (as the accustomed phrase goes) 'a mere shadow of her former self.' (2) Just as a solid body, lighted by the sun, casts, as a necessary concomitant, a shadow of itself, so a sound, omitted under the requisite conditions, casts an echo of itself: echo is, in relation to sound, the same sort of thing as shadow in relation to substance.

11. 8, 9. *A drear Murmur, between their songs, is all the woodmen hear.* Echo will not now repeat the songs of the woodmen: she merely murmurs some snatches of the 'remembered lay' of Adonais.

Stanza 16, 1. 1. *Grief made the young Spring wild.* This introduction of Spring may be taken as implying that Shelley supposed Keats to have died in the Spring: but in fact he died in the Winter—February 23. As to this point see pp. 31 and 97.

11. 1–3. *And she threw down Her kindling buds, as if she Autumn were, Or they dead leaves.* This corresponds to a certain extent with the phrases in Bion, 'the flowers are withered up with grief,' and 'yea all the flowers are faded' (p. 68); and in Moschus, 'and in sorrow for thy fall the trees cast down their fruit, and all the flowers have faded' (p. 69). It may be worth observing that Shelley says—'As if she Autumn were, *or* they dead leaves' (not '*and* they dead leaves'). He therefore seems to present the act of Spring from two separate points of view; (1) She threw

down the buds, as if she had been Autumn, whose office it is to throw down, and not to cherish and develop; (2) she threw down the buds as if they had been, not buds of the nascent year, but such dead leaves of the olden year as still linger on the spray when Spring arrives.

11. 5–7. ***To Phoebus was not Hyacinth so dear, Nor to himself Narcissus, as to both Thou, Adonais; wan they stand and sere,*** &c. This passage assimilates two sections in the Elegy of Moschus, p. 69: 'Now, thou hyacinth, whisper the letters on thee graven, and add a deeper ai ai to thy petals: he is dead, the beautiful singer. . . . Nor so much did pleasant Lesbos mourn for Alcaeus,' &c. The passage of Shelley is rather complicated in its significance, because it mixes up the personages Hyacinthus and Narcissus with the flowers hyacinth and narcissus. The beautiful youth Hyacinthus was dear to Phoebus: on his untimely death (he was slain by a quoit which Phoebus threw, and which the jealous Zephyrus blew aside so that it struck Hyacinthus on the head), the god changed his blood into the flower hyacinth, which bears markings interpreted by the Grecian fancy into the lettering *ai ai* (alas, alas!). The beautiful youth Narcissus, contemplating himself in a streamlet, became enamoured of his own face, and, pining away, was converted into the flower narcissus. This accounts for the lines, 'To Phoebus was not Hyacinth so dear, Nor to himself Narcissus.' But, when we come to the sequence, 'as to both Thou, Adonais,' we have to do no longer with the youths Hyacinthus and Narcissus, but with the flowers hyacinth and narcissus; it a the flowers which (according to Shelley) loved Adonais better than the youths were loved, the one by Phoebus and the other by himself. These flowers—being some of the kindling buds which Spring had thrown down—stand 'wan and sere.' (This last point is rather the reverse of a phrase in Bion's Elegy, p. 68, 'The flowers flush red for anguish.') It may perhaps be held that the transition from the youths to the flowers, and from the emotions of Phoebus and of Narcissus to those assigned to the flowers, is not very happily managed by Shelley: it is artificial, and not free from confusion. As to the hyacinth, the reader will readily perceive that a flower which bears markings read off into *ai ai* (or AI AI seems more correct) cannot be the same which we now call hyacinth. Ovid says that in form the hyacinth resembles a lily, and that its colour is 'purpureus,' or deep red. John Martyn, who published in 1755 ***The Georgicks of Virgil with an English***

Translation, has an elaborate note on the subject. He concludes thus: 'I am pretty well satisfied that the flower celebrated by the poets is what we now are acquainted with under the name 'Lilium floribus reflexis,' or Martagon, and perhaps may be that very species which we call Imperial Martagon. The flowers of most sorts of martagons have many spots of a deeper colour: and sometimes I have seen these spots run together in such a manner as to form the letters AI in several places.' Shelley refers to the hyacinth in another passage (*Prometheus Unbound,* ii. 1) which seems to indicate that he regarded the antique hyacinth as being the same as the modern hyacinth,—

'As the *blue bells*
Of hyacinth tell Apollo's written grief.'

1. 8. *Amid the faint companions of their youth.* In Shelley's edition the words are 'Amid the drooping comrades,' &c. The change was made under the same circumstances as noted on p. 108. Whether it is a change for the better may admit of some question. The faint companions of the youth of the hyacinth and the narcissus must be other flowers, such as Spring had thrown down.

1. 9. With dew all turned to tears,—odour, to sighing ruth. *The dew upon the hyacinth and narcissus is converted into tears: they exhale sighs, instead of fragrance. All this is in rather a* falsetto tone. It has some resemblance to the more simple and touching phrase in the Elegy by Moschus (p. 69): 'Ye flowers, now in sad clusters breathe yourselves away.'

Stanza 17, 11. 1, 2. *Thy spirit's sister, the lorn nightingale, Mourns not her mate,* &c. The reason for calling the nightingale the sister of the spirit of Keats (Adonais) does not perhaps go beyond this—that, as the nightingale is a supreme songster among birds, so was Keats a supreme songster among men. It is possible however—and one willingly supposes so—that Shelley singled out the nightingale for mention, in recognition of the consummate beauty of Keats's *Ode to the Nightingale,* published in the same volume with *Hyperion.* The epithet 'lorn' may also be noted in the same connexion; as Keats's Ode terminates with a celebrated passage in which 'forlorn' is the leading word (but not as an epithet for the nightingale itself)—

'Forlorn!—the very word is as a knell,' &c.

Keats does not seem to contemplate the nightingale as a 'lorn' or distressful bird, but as one that sings 'of summer in full-throated ease,' and yet (as at the end of the Ode) with a 'plaintive anthem.' The nightingale is also introduced into the Elegy of Moschus for Bion: 'Ye nightingales that lament,' &c. (p. 69), and 'Nor ever sang so sweet the nightingale on the cliffs.' Poets are fond of speaking of the nightingale as being the hen-bird and Shelley follows this precedent. It is a fallacy, for the songster is always the cock-bird.

1. 3. ***Not so the eagle,*** &c. The general statement in these lines is that Albion wails for the death of Keats more melodiously than the nightingale mourning for her lost mate, and more passionately than the eagle robbed of her young. This statement has proved true enough in the long run: when Shelley wrote it was only prospectively or potentially true, for the death of Keats excited no immediate widespread concern in England. It should be observed that, by introducing Albion as a figurative personage in his Elegy, Shelley disregards his emblematic Grecian youth Adonais, and goes straight to the actual Englishman Keats. This passage, taken as a whole, is related to that of Moschus (p. 69) regarding the nightingale, the sea-bird, and the bird of Memnon; see also the passage, 'and not for Sappho, but still for thee,' &c.

11. 4, 5. ***Could nourish in the sun's domain Her mighty youth with morning.*** This phrase seems to have some analogy to that of Milton in his ***Areopagitica*** : 'Methinks I see in my mind a noble and puissant nation rousing herself like a strong man after sleep and shaking her invincible locks. Methinks I see her as an eagle muing her mighty youth, and kindling her undazzled eyes at the full mid-day beam—purging and unsealing her long-abused sight at the fountain itself of heavenly radiance.' Cp. in ***Hellas*** : 'As an eagle fed with morning.' The image which follows, of

the eagle's wrath over her empty nest, was suggested by Aeschylus, *Agamemnon* 49–56:—

as that passage was suggested by *Odyssey* xvi. 216:—

11. 7, 8. *The curse of Cain Light on his head,* &c. An imprecation against the critic of Keats's *Endymion* in the *Quarterly Review* : see especially p. 41, &c. The curse of Cain was that he should be 'a fugitive and a vagabond,' as well as unsuccessful in tilling the soil. Shelley probably pays no attention to these details, but simply means 'the curse for murder.'

Stanza 18, 11. 1, 2. *Ah woe is me! Winter is come and gone, But grief returns with the revolving year,* &c. See the passage in Moschus (p. 69): 'Ah me! when the mallows wither,' &c. The phrase in Bion has also a certain but restricted analogy to this stanza: 'Thou must again bewail him, again must weep for him another year' (p. 69). As to the phrase 'Winter is come and gone,' see the note (p. 115) on 'Grief made the young Spring wild.'

1. 5. Fresh leaves and flowers deck the dead Seasons' bier. This phrase is barely consistent with the statement (st. 16) as to Spring throwing down her kindling buds. Perhaps, moreover, it was an error of print to give 'Seasons' in the plural: 'Season's' (meaning winter) would seem more accurate. A somewhat similar idea is conveyed in one of Shelley's lyrics, *Autumn, a Dirge,* written in 1820:—

'And the Year
On the earth her death-bed, in a shroud of leaves dead,
Is lying.'

1. 7. *Brere.* An antiquated form of the word brier.

1. 9. *Like unimprisoned flames.* Flames which, after being pent up within some substance or space, finally find a vent.

Stanza 19, 1. 2. ***A quickening life,*** &c. The present stanza is generally descriptive of the effects of Springtime upon the earth. This reawakening of Nature (Shelley says) has always taken place, in annual recurrence, since 'the great morning of the world when first God dawned on chaos.' This last expression must be construed with a certain latitude. The change from an imagined chaos into a divinely-ordered cosmos is not necessarily coincident with the interchange of seasons, and especially the transition from Winter to Spring, upon the planet Earth. All that can be safely propounded on such a subject is that the sequence of seasons is a constant and infallible phenomenon of Nature in that condition of our planet with which alone we have, or can have, any acquaintance. So in ***Hellas*** :—

'In the great morning of the world
The Spirit of God with might unfurled
The flag of Freedom over Chaos.'

(See a paper by Mr. T. J. Wise. Shelley Society.) With the whole of this stanza and the next should be compared the lines to Venus as the quickening power, with which Lucretius opens his poem (i. 6–9):—

'Te, dea, te fugiunt venti, te nubila caeli
Adventumque tuum; tibi suavis daedala tellus
Summittit flores; tibi rident aequora ponti,
Placatumque nitet diffuso lumine caelum.'

1. 5. ***In its steam immersed,*** i. e. in the steam—or vapour or exhalation—of the 'quickening life.'

Stanza. 20, 11. 1, 2. ***The leprous corpse, touched by this spirit tender, Exhales itself in flowers of gentle breath.*** 'This spirit tender' is the 'quickening life' of the renascent year; or briefly the Spring. By 'the leprous corpse' Shelley may mean, not the corpse of an actual leper, but any corpse in a loathsome state of decay. Even so abhorrent an object avails to fertilize the soil, and thus promotes the growth of odorous flowers.

1. 3. ***Like incarnations of the stars,*** &c. These flowers—star-like blossoms—illumine death and the grave: the light which would belong to them as stars is converted into the fragrance proper to them as flowers. This image is rather confused, and I think rather stilted: moreover, 'incarnation' (or embodiment flesh in flesh is hardly the right word for the vegetative nature of flowers. As forms of life, the flowers mock or deride the grave-worm which battens or makes merry on corruption. The appropriateness of the term 'merry worm' seems very disputable. Cp. Hamlet's 'a certain convocation of politic worms' (***Hamlet,*** iv. 3). Here the alliterations help to give point to the words.

1. 6. ***Nought we know dies.*** This affirmation springs directly out of the consideration just presented to us—that even the leprous corpse does not, through various stages of decay, pass into absolute nothingness: on the contrary, its constituents take new forms, and subserve a re-growth of life, as in the flowers which bedeck the grave. From this single and impressive instance the poet passes to the general and unfailing law—No material object of which we have cognizance really dies: all such objects are in a perpetual cycle of change. This conception has been finely developed in a brace of early poems of Lord Tennyson, ***All Things will Die,*** and ***Nothing will Die*** :—

'The stream will cease to flow,
The wind will cease to blow,
The clouds will cease to fleet,
The heart will cease to beat—
For all things must die.

'The stream flows,
The wind blows,
The cloud fleets,
The heart beats,
Nothing will die.
Nothing will die;

All things will change
Through eternity.'

Cp. also **Romeo and Juliet,** ii. 3:—

'The earth, that's Nature's mother, is her tomb;
What is her burying grave, that is her womb.

And Aeschylus, **Choeph.** 127–8:—

Also Lucretius, ii. 990–1010.

11. 6–8. ***Shall that alone which knows Be as a sword consumed before the sheath By sightless lightning?*** From the axiom 'Nought we know dies'—an axiom which should be understood as limited to what we call material objects (which Shelley however considered to be indistinguishable, in essence, from ideas, see p. 57)—he proceeds to the question, 'Shall that alone which knows'—i. e. shall the mind alone—die and be annihilated? If the mind were to die, while the body continues extant (not indeed in the form of a human body, but in various phases of ulterior development), then the mind would resemble a sword which, by the action of lightning, is consumed (molten, dissolved) within its sheath, while the sheath itself remains unconsumed. This is put as a question, and Shelley does not supply an answer to it here, though the terms in which his inquiry is couched seem intended to suggest a reply to the effect that the mind shall ***not*** die. The meaning of the epithet 'sightless,' as applied to lightning, seems disputable. Of course the primary sense of this word is 'not-seeing, blind'; but Shelley would probably not have scrupled to use it in the sense of 'unseen.' I incline to suppose that Shelley means 'unseen'; not so much that the lightning is itself unseen as that its action in fusing the sword, which remains concealed within the sheath, is unseen. But the more obvious sense of 'blind, unregardful,' could also be justified. The image of these lines is illustrated by a passage in the ***Defence of Poetry,*** where, after speaking of passionless poets, such as Addison, Shelley continues: 'Poetry is a sword of lightning, ever unsheath'd, which consumes the scabbard that would contain it.' To recur to

the epithet 'sightless.' Among the many epithets used by Shelley of lightning are 'silent' (**Adonais,** st. 25), 'voiceless' (**Mont Blanc,** st. 5), 'blind' (**Cenci,** v. 4. 107), 'invisible' (**Epipsychidion,** 399). The two last, and still more clearly the line 'Like lightning that flash'd and died' (**We met,** ii. 2), may perhaps help us to understand 'sightless' here, at least in one aspect of the term. The lightning is invisible as soon as it has done its work.

11. 8, 9. *Th' intense atom glows A moment, then is quenched in a most cold repose.* The term 'th' intense atom' is a synonym for 'that which knows,' or the mind. By death it is 'quenched in a most cold repose': but the repose is not necessarily extinction.

Stanza 21. The thought of the later lines of this stanza is well illustrated by Lucretius, ii. 578–581:—

'Nec nox ulla diem neque noctem aurora secutast
quae non audierit mixtos vagitibus aegris
ploratus mortis comites et funeris atri.'

11. 1, 2. *Alas that all we loved of him should be, But for our grief, as if it had not been.* 'All we loved of him' must be the mind and character—the mental and personal endowments—of Adonais: his bodily frame is little or not at all in question here. By these lines therefore Shelley seems to intimate that the mind or soul of Adonais is indeed now and for ever extinct: it lives no longer save in the grief of the survivors. But it does not follow that this is a final expression of Shelley's conviction on the subject: the passage should be read as in context with the whole poem.

11. 5, 6. *Great and mean Meet massed in death, who lends what life must borrow.* The meaning of the last words is far from clear to me. I think Shelley may intend to say that, in this our mortal state, death is the solid and permanent fact; it is rather a world of death than of life. The phenomena of life are but like a transitory loan from the great emporium, death. Shelley no doubt wanted a rhyme for 'morrow' and 'sorrow': he has made use of 'borrow' in a compact but not perspicu-

ous phrase.

Stanza 22, 1. 2. '*Wake thou,' cried Misery, 'childless Mother!* ' We here return
to Urania, of whom we had last heard in st. 6. See the passage translated by Shelley
from Bion (p. 67). 'Sleep no more, Venus: . . . 'tis Misery calls,' &c.; but here the
phrase, ''Tis Misery calls,' is Shelley's own. He more than once introduces Misery
(in the sense of Unhappiness, Tribulation) as an emblematic personage. There is his
lyric named *Misery,* written in 1818, which begins—

'Come, be happy,—sit by me,
Shadow-vested Misery:
Coy, unwilling, silent bride,
Mourning in thy robe of pride,
Desolation deified.'

There is also the briefer lyric named *Death,* 1817, which begins—

'They die—the dead return not. Misery
Sits near an open grave, and calls them over,
A youth with hoary hair and haggard eye.'

11. 3, 4. '*Slake in thy heart's core A wound more fierce than his, with tears
and sighs.* ' Construe: 'Slake with tears and sighs a wound in thy heart's core—a
wound more fierce than his.' See (p. 102) the remarks, apposite to st. 4, upon the use
of inversion by Shelley.

1. 5. *All the Dreams that watched Urania's eyes.* We had not hitherto heard
of 'Dreams' in connexion with Urania, but only in connexion with Adonais himself.
These 'Dreams that watched Urania's eyes' appear to be dreams in the more obvious
sense of that word—visions which had haunted the slumbers of Urania.

1. 8. *Swift as a thought by the snake memory stung.* The context suggests
that the 'thought' here in question is a grievous thought, and the term 'the snake

memory' conveys therefore a corresponding impression of pain. Shelley however had not the usual feeling of repulsion or abhorrence for snakes and serpents. Various passages could be cited to prove this; more especially canto 1 of the **Revolt of Islam,** where the Spirit of Good is figured under the form of a serpent: see also 'the golden snake,' stanza 18.

1. 9. *From her ambrosial rest the fading Splendour sprung.* Urania. She is in her own nature a splendour, or celestial deity: at the present moment her brightness is 'fading,' as being overcast by sorrow and dismay, or else the epithet is to be accepted as anticipating what is more fully developed in the next stanza. 'Her ambrosial rest' does not appear to signify anything more precise than 'her rest, proper to an immortal being.' The forms 'sprung, sung,' &c. are constantly used by Shelley instead of 'sprang, sang,' &c.

Stanza 23, 1. 5. *Had left the Earth a corpse.* Shelley, in this quasi-Greek poem, takes no count of the fact that the sun, when it ceases to illumine one part of the earth, is shining upon another part. He treats the unillumined part as if it were the whole earth—which has hereby become 'a corpse.'

Stanza 24, 11. 1, 2. *Out of her secret Paradise she sped, Through camps and cities,* &c. 'Secret' has here the sense (as in Latin) of 'secluded.' In highly figurative language, this stanza pictures the passage of Urania to the death-chamber of Adonais in Rome, as if the spiritual essence and external form of the goddess were wounded by the uncongenial atmosphere of human malice and detraction through which she has to pass. The whole description is spiritualized from that of Bion (p. 67):—

'Wildered, ungirt, unsandalled—the thorns pierce
Her hastening feet, and drink her sacred blood.'

1. 3. *And human hearts.* These words come as a *surprise* in the climax, stone—steel—human hearts. This figure is common in satirical poets, and conveys a meaning sometimes playful, sometimes, as here, bitter.

11. 4, 5. *The invisible Palms of her tender feet.* Shelley more than once uses 'palms' for 'soles' of the feet. See *Prometheus Unbound,* iv:—

'Our feet now, every palm,
Are sandalled with calm';

and *The Triumph of Life* :—

'As she moved under the mass
Of the deep cavern, and, with palms so tender
Their tread broke not the mirror of the billow,
Glided along the river.'

Perhaps Shelley got this usage from the Italian: in that language the web-feet of aquatic birds are termed 'palme.'

11. 8, 9. *Whose sacred blood, like the young tears of May, Paved with eternal flowers that undeserving way.* The tears of May are rain-drops; young, because the year is not far advanced. 'That undeserving way' seems a very poor expression. See (p. 68) the passage from Bion: 'A tear the Paphian sheds for each blood-drop of Adonis, and tears and blood on the earth are turned to flowers.'

Stanza 25, 11. 1–3. *Death . . . Blushed to annihilation.* This very daring hyperbole will hardly bear—nor does it want—manipulation into prose. Briefly, the nature of Death is to be pallid: therefore Death, in blushing, abnegates his very nature, and almost ceases to be Death.

11. 3, 4. *The breath Revisited those lips,* &c. As Death tended towards 'annihilation,' so Adonais tended towards revival.

1. 7. '*Silent lightning.* ' Lightning unaccompanied by thunder—summer lightning. See above on stanza 20, 11. 6–8.

Stanza 26, 1. 1. '***Stay yet awhile.*** ' See Bion (p. 68): 'Stay, Adonis! stay, dearest one!'

1. 2. '***Kiss me, so long but as a kiss may live.*** ' See as above:—

'That I may kiss thee now for the last time—
But for as long as one short kiss may live!'

1. 3. '***My heartless breast.*** ' Urania's breast is heartless, in the sense that, having bestowed her whole heart upon Adonais, she has none to bestow upon any one else: so I understand the epithet.

1. 4. '***That word, that kiss, shall all thoughts else survive,*** ' &c. See Bion (p. 68): 'This kiss will I treasure,' &c.

11. 7–9. 'I would give All that I am, to be as thou now art:—But I am chained to Time, and cannot thence depart. ' Founded on Bion (p. 68): 'While wretched I yet live, being a goddess, and may not follow thee.' The Alteration of phrase is somewhat remarkable. In Bion's Elegy the Cyprian Aphrodite is 'a goddess,' and therefore immoral. In Shelley's Elegy the Uranian Aphrodite does not speak of herself under any designation of immortality or eternity, but as 'chained to ***Time,*** ' and incapable of departing from Time. As long as Time lives and operates, Urania must do the same. The dead have escaped from the dominion of Time: this Urania cannot do. There is a somewhat similar train of thought in ***Prometheus Unbound,*** where Prometheus the Titan, after enduring the torture of the Furies (i.), says—

'Peace is in the grave:
The grave holds all things beautiful and good.
I am a God, and cannot find it ***there.*** '

Stanza 27, 11. 1–4. '***O gentle child, beautiful as thou wert, Why didst thou*** *leave,* ' &c. This is founded on—and as usual spiritualized from—the passage in Bion (p. 68): 'For why, ah overbold! Didst thou follow the chase, and, being so fair, why wert thou thus over-hardy to fight with beasts?'

1. 4. '***Dare the unpastured dragon in his den.*** ' This phrase must no doubt be interpreted, not only in relation to the figurative Adonais, but also to the actual Keats. Keats had dared the unpastured dragon in his den, in the sense that he made a bold adventure into the poetical field, under conditions certain to excite the ire of adherents of the old school, whether in literature or in politics. For 'unpastured' cp. ***Prometheus Unbound,*** iii. 2:—

'It is the unpastured sea, hungering for calm.'

The epithet is Greek in form (cp. of the bee in ***Anthol. Pal.*** vi. 239). Shelley may have had in mind the language used about Leviathan in the Book of Job, ch. xli.

1. 6. '***Wisdom the mirrored shield, or scorn the spear.*** ' Urania arraigns Keats for having made his inroad upon the dragon, unguarded by wisdom or by scorn. His want of wisdom was shown (we may assume) by the grave blemishes and extravagances which mark its composition, and wantonly invited attack. His want of scorn was (according to Shelley's view of the facts) clear enough: he had not been equal to despising a spiteful attack, but had fretted himself to death under it. Shelley was probably thinking in the first place of Perseus, who, armed with a bright shield by Athene, and a scimitar by Hermes, cut off the head of Medusa, watching her reflection in the mirror-shield, since a look from the monster herself would have turned him into stone. The story is told by Ovid, ***Melam.*** iv. 770–791, and Lucan, ix. 659–684. In Ariosto (***Orlando Furioso,*** ii. 55; xxxii. 75) we read of a magic shield casting a supernatural and intolerable splendour, whereby every gazer (including a sea-monster) is cast into a trance; and of a spear whose lightest touch overthrows every opponent. Compare the shield of Arthur in the ***Faery Queen,*** Book I, canto vii. 33, and canto viii. 19. The spear may well symbolize scorn, and is the appropriate weapon for dealing with mean enemies; cp. Ithuriel's spear in ***Paradise Lost,***

Book VII. In Lucian's dialogue between Eros and Aphrodite, Eros complains that he has no power against Athene alone of goddesses, since besides the terrors of her majestic demeanour and her shield (not here a mirror-shield), he would be at once transfixed by her spear.

11. 7, 8. '*The full cycle when Thy spirit should have filled its crescent sphere.*' The spirit of Keats is here assimilated to the moon, which grows from a crescent into a disk-like form.

1. 9. '*The monsters of life's waste.*' The noxious creatures which infest the wilderness of human life. As Shelley had in the previous line referred to the moon (Diana), it seems possible that he here again refers to Diana in her character of a huntress; and an allusion to Diana involves a kind of allusion to Keats's *Endymion.*

Stanza 28, 1. 1. '*The herded wolves,*' &c. These same 'monsters' are now pictured under three aspects. They are herded wolves, which will venture lo pursue a traveller, but will not face him if he turns upon them boldly; and obscene ravens, which make an uproar over dead bodies, or dead reputations; and vultures, which follow in the wake of a conqueror, and gorge upon that which is already overthrown. In the succeeding stanza, 29, two other epithetal similes are bestowed upon the monsters—they become 'reptiles' and 'ephemeral insects.' All these repulsive images are of course here applied to critics of wilfully obtuse or malignant mind, such as Shelley accounted the *Quarterly* reviewer of Keats to be. The epithet 'obscene' is applied by Latin poets to birds and other creatures of sinister omen. So in *Aen.* xii. 876, &c.

1. 5. '*And whose wings rain contagion.*' Cp. Marlowe's *Jew of Malta,* ii. 1:—

'Thus, like the sad presaging raven, that . . .
Doth shake contagion from her sable wings.'

11. 5, 6. '*How they fled, When like Apollo,*' &c. The allusion is to perfectly

well-known incidents in the opening poetic career of Lord Byron. His lordship, in earliest youth, published a very insignificant volume of verse named **Hours of Idleness.** The **Edinburgh Review** —rightly in substance, but with some superfluous harshness of tone—pronounced this volume to be poor stuff. Byron retaliated by producing his satire entitled **English Bards and Scotch Reviewers.** With this book he scored a success. His next publication was the generally and enthusiastically admired commencement of **Childe Harold,** 1812; after which date the critics justly acclaimed him as a poet—although in course of time they grew lavishly severe upon him from the point of view of morals and religion. I reproduce from the Pisan edition the punctuation—'When like Apollo, from his golden bow'; but I think the exact sense would be better brought out if we read—'When, like Apollo from his golden bow, The Pythian,' &c.

11. 7, 8. ' *The Pythian of the age one arrow sped, And smiled.* ' Byron is here assimilated to Apollo Pythius—Apollo the Python-slayer. The statue named Apollo Belvedere has been regarded as representing the god at the moment after he has discharged his arrow at the python (serpent), his countenance irradiated with a half-smile of divine scorn and triumph. In recent years, however, various writers of credit have held that the action of Apollo in this statue is truly that of holding the aegis in battle. The terms employed by Shelley seem to glance more particularly at this celebrated statue: which was the more appropriate as Byron had devoted to the same figure two famous stanzas in the 4th canto of **Childe Harold** —

'Or view the Lord of the unerring bow,
The God of life and poesy and light,' &c.

1. 9. ' *They fawn on the proud feet that spurn them lying low.* ' In the Pisan edition we read 'that spurn them as they go.' No doubt the change (introduced as in other instances named on pp. 108 and 116) must be Shelley's own. The picture presented to the mind is more consistent, according to the altered reading. The critics, as we are told in this stanza, had at first 'fled' from Byron's arrow: afterwards they 'fawned on his proud feet.' In order to do this, they must have paused in their flight, and returned; and, in the act of fawning on Byron's feet, they must have crouched

down, or were 'lying low.' (Mr. Forman, in his edition of Shelley, pointed this out.) With the words 'as they go' the image was not self-consistent: for the critics could not be 'going,' or walking away, at the same time when they were fawning on the poet's feet. This last remark assumes that the words 'as they go' mean 'as the critics go': but perhaps (and indeed I think this is more than probable) the real meaning was 'as the feet of Byron go'—as Byron proceeds disdainfully on his way. If this was Shelley's original meaning, he probably observed after a while that the words 'as **they** go' seem to follow on with '**they** fawn,' and not with 'the proud feet'; and, in order to remove the ambiguity, he substituted the expression 'lying low.'

Stanza 29, 11. 1–3. '*The sun comes forth, and many reptiles spawn; He sets, and each ephemeral insect then Is gathered into death.* ' The spawning of a reptile (say a lizard or toad), and the death of an insect (say a beetle or gnat), are two things totally unconnected. Shelley however seems, on the first reading, to link them together, as if this spawning were the origin of the life, the brief life, of the insect. He might thus appear to use 'reptile,' not in the defined sense which we commonly attach to the word, but in general sense of 'a creeping creature,' such for instance as a grub or caterpillar, the first form of an insect, leading on to its final metamorphosis or development. His natural history would then be curiously at fault: for no grub or caterpillar can spawn—which is the function of the fully-developed insect itself, whether 'ephemeral' or otherwise. Probably the full meaning is: 'When the sun rises, reptiles spawn and insects come forth; when he sets, the reptiles (i. e. the meanest creeping things) and the insects die for ever.' But Shelley, by an economy not uncommon with poets, has only given one term of each statement: 'When the sun rises, reptiles spawn; when the sun sets, insects die.' It is not exact to say that 'reptiles spawn,' if the meaning is that young reptiles come out of yesterday's spawn.

1. 4. '*And the immortal stars awake again.* ' The imagery of this stanza (apart from the 'reptiles' and 'ephemeral insects') deserves a little consideration. The sun (says Shelley) arises, and then sets; when it sets, the immortal stars awake again. Similarly, a godlike mind (say the mind of Keats) appears, and its light illumines the earth, and veils the heaven: when it disappears, 'the spirit's awful night' is left to 'its kindred lamps.' This seems as much as to say that the splendour of a new poetic

genius appears to contemporaries to throw preceding poets into obscurity; but this is only a matter of the moment, for, when the new genius sinks in death, the others shine forth again as stars of the intellectual zenith, to which the new genius is kindred indeed, but not superior; but meanwhile the swarms of gnats, which depended upon the sun for their life, though they dimmed his brightness, die. With these words concludes the speech of Urania, which began in stanza 25.

Stanza 30, 1. 1. *The Mountain Shepherds.* These are contemporary British poets, whom Shelley represents as mourning the death of Keats. Shepherds are such familiar figures in poetry—utilized for instance in Milton's *Lycidas,* as well as by many poets of antiquity—that the introduction of them into Shelley's Elegy is no matter for surprise. As to the term '*mountain* shepherds,' Shelley may have written with a certain degree of reference to that couplet in *Lycidas* —

'For we were nursed upon the self-same *hill,*
Fed the same flock, by fountain, shade, and rill.'

In the celebrated pastoral of Sannazzaro, the *Arcadia,* the scene is 'on the summit of Parthenius, a mount not low in pastoral Arcadia'; and we are told, 'In this spot the shepherds with their flocks are often wont to meet from the neighbouring mounts.'

1. 2. *Their garlands sere, their magic mantles rent.* The garlands or chaplets of the mountain shepherds have become sere because (it may be presumed) the wearers, in their grief for the mortal illness and death of Adonais, have for some little while left them unrenewed. Or possibly the garlands withered at the moment when Spring 'threw down her kindling buds' (stanza 16). I do not well understand the expression 'magic mantles.' There seems to be no reason why the mantles of the shepherds, considered as shepherds, should be magic. Even when we contemplate the shepherds as poets, we may fail to discern why any magical property should be assigned to their mantles. Perhaps we should understand that the shepherds wore mantles, which, when we convert the shepherds into poets, can be regarded as their 'singing-robes,' comparable to black robes embroidered with mystic charac-

ters, proper to magicians. Shelley would thus have intended to bridge over the gap between the nominal shepherds and the real poets, viewed as inspired singers: for this purpose he has adopted a bold verbal expedient, but not I think an efficient one. It may be noticed that the 'uncouth swain' who is represented in *Lycidas* as singing the dirge (in other words, Milton himself) is spoken of as having a mantle—it is a 'mantle blue' (see the penultimate line of that poem). Cp. 'magic tone,' said of Keats's poetry in stanza 36.

1. 3. *The Pilgrim of Eternity.* This is Lord Byron. As inventor of the personage Childe Harold, the hero and so-called 'Pilgrim' of the poem *Childe Harold's Pilgrimage,* and as being himself to a great extent identical with his hero, Byron was frequently termed 'the Pilgrim.' Shelley adopts this designation, which he magnifies into 'the Pilgrim of Eternity.' He admired Byron most enthusiastically as a poet, and was generally on easy—sometimes on cordial—terms with him as a man. He has left us a fine and discriminating portrait of Byron in the 'Count Maddalo' of his poem *Julian and Maddalo,* written in 1818. At times, however, Shelley felt and expressed great indignation against Byron, especially in reference to the ungenerous and cruel conduct of the latter towards Miss Clairmont. See some brief reference to this matter at p. 9.

11. 3–5. *Whose fame Over his living head like heaven is bent, An early but enduring monument.* These phrases are not very definite. When fame is spoken of as being bent over Byron's head, we must conceive of fame as taking a form cognizable by the senses. I think Shelley means to assimilate it to the rainbow; saying substantially—Fame is like an arc bent over Byron's head, as the arc of the rainbow is bent over the expanse of heaven. The ensuing term 'monument' applies rather to fame in the abstract than to any image of fame as an arc.

11. 6, 7. *Came, veiling all the lightnings of his song In sorrow.* No doubt it would have been satisfactory to Shelley if he could have found that Byron entertained or expressed any serious concern at Keats's premature death, and at the hard measure which had been meted out to him by critics. Byron did in fact admire *Hyperion;* writing (in November 1821, not long after the publication of *Adon-*

ais)—'His fragment of **Hyperion** seems actually inspired by the Titans, and is as sublime as Aeschylus'; and other utterances of his show that—being with difficulty persuaded to suppose that Keats's health and life had succumbed to the attack in the **Quarterly** —he fittingly censured the want of feeling or want of reflection on the critic's part which had produced such a result. But on the whole Byron's feeling towards Keats was one of savage contempt during the young poet's life, and of bantering levity after his death. Here are some specimens. (From a letter to Mr. Murray, October 12, 1820.) 'There is such a trash of Keats and the like upon my tables that I am ashamed to look at them . . . No more Keats, I entreat. Flay him alive: if some of you don't, I must skin him myself. There is no bearing the drivelling idiotism of the manikin.'

' "Who killed John Keats?"
"I," says the Quarterly,
So savage and Tartarly;
" 'Twas one of my feats."'
'John Keats, who was killed off by one critique
Just as he really promised something great
If not intelligible, without Greek
Contrived to talk about the gods of late,
Much as they might have been supposed to speak.
Poor fellow, his was an untoward fate!
'Tis strange the mind, that very fiery particle,
Should let itself be snuffed out by an article.'

11. 7–9. *From her wilds Ierne sent The sweetest lyrist of her saddest wrong, And love taught grief to fall like music from his tongue.* Ierne (Ireland) sent Thomas Moore, the lyrist of her wrongs—an allusion to the *Irish Melodies,* and some other poems. There is not, I believe, any evidence to show that Moore took the slightest interest in Keats, his doings or his fate: Shelley is responsible for Moore's love, grief, and music, in this connexion. A letter from Keats has been published showing that at one time he expected to meet Moore personally (see p. 47). Whether he did so or not I cannot say for certain, but I apprehend not: the published Diary of Moore, of

about the same date, suggests the negative.

Stanza 31, 1. 1. '*Midst others of less note.* Shelley clearly means 'less note' than Byron and Moore—not less note than the 'one frail form.'

1. 1. *Came one frail Form,* &c. This personage represents Shelley himself. Shelley here describes himself under a profusion of characteristics, briefly defined: it may be interesting to summarize them, apart from the other details with which they are interspersed. He is a frail form; a phantom among men; companionless; one who had gazed Actaeon-like on Nature's naked loveliness, and who now fled with feeble steps, hounded by his own thoughts; a pard-like spirit beautiful and swift; a love masked in desolation; a power begirt with weakness, scarcely capable of lifting the weight of the hour; a breaking billow, which may even now be broken; the last of the company, neglected and apart—a herd-abandoned deer struck by the hunter's dart; in Keats's fate, he wept his own; his brow was branded and ensanguined. Most of these attributes can be summed up under one heading—that of extreme sensitiveness and susceptibility, which meet with no response of sustainment, but rather with misjudgement, repulse, and outrage. Some readers may think that Shelley insists upon this aspect of his characters to a degree rather excessive, and dangerously near the confines of feminine sensibility, rather than virile fortitude. Apart from this predominant type of character, Shelley describes his spirit as 'beautiful and swift'—which surely it was: and he says that, having gazed upon Nature's naked loveliness, he has suffered the fate of a second Actaeon, fleeing 'o'er the world's wilderness,' and persued by his own thoughts like raging hounds. By this expression Shelley apparently means that he had over-boldly tried to fathom the depths of things and of mind, but, baffled and dismayed in the effort, suffered, as a man living among men, by the very tension and vividness of his thoughts, and their daring in the expression. See what he says of himself, in prose, on p. 93.

11. 4, 5. *He, as I guess, Had gazed,* &c. The use of the verb 'guess' in the sense of 'to surmise, conjecture, infer,' is now mostly counted as an Americanism. This is not correct; for the verb has often been thus used by standard English authors. Such a practice was not however common in England in Shelley's time, and he may have

been guided chiefly by the rhyming.

Stanza 32, 1. 4. ***The weight of the superincumbent hour.*** This line is scarcely rhythmical: to bring it within the ordinary scheme of rhythm, one would have to lay an exaggerated stress on two of its syllables—'the superincumbent,' Neither this treatment of the line, nor the line itself apart from this treatment, can easily be justified.

Stanza 33, 11. 1, 2. ***His head was bound with pansies overblown, And faded violets.*** The pansy (pensée) is the flower of thought, or memory: we commonly call it heartsease, but Shelley no doubt uses it here with a different, or indeed contrary, meaning. The violet indicates, according to some authorities, fidelity, according to others, modesty. A stanza from one of his lyrics may be appropriately cited—***Remembrance,*** dated 1821:—

'Lilies for a bridal bed,
Roses for a matron's head,
Violets for a maiden dead,
Pansies let ***my*** flowers be.
On the living grave I bear
Scatter them without a tear;
Let no friend, however dear,
Waste a hope, a fear, for me.'

See also ***Hamlet,*** iv. 5 (Ophelia loq.): 'And there is pansies, that's for thoughts. . . . There's a daisy. I would give you some violets; but they withered all, when my father died.' Mrs. Shelley writes July 26, 1822: 'In a little poem of his are these words: "Pansies let my flowers be." Pansies are heartsease; and in another he says that pansies mean memory.'

1. 3. Shelley here represents himself as bearing the thyrsus or Bacchic wand— 'The thyrsus was a light wand with its head covered with a bunch of ivy or vine-leaves, or the cone of a fir-tree, or with cone and leaves combined. Sometimes a

sharp spike was imbedded in the upper part of the stick.' (Sandys' note on Eurip-ides, **Bacchae** 25.) The ivy was the poet's emblem:—

'Me doctarum hederae praemia frontium
dis miscent superis.' (Horace, **Od.** i. 1. 29–30.)

The thyrsus was appropriate to poets, as well as to Bacchanals, cp. Lucretius (i. 922–3):—

'nec me animi fallit quam sint obscura; sed acri
percussit thyrso laudis spes magna meum cor.'

To the usual foliage of the thyrsus Shelley has added the mourning cypress.

1. 9. *A herd-abandoned deer.* Cp. *As You Like It,* ii. 1:—

'To the which place a poor sequestered stag,
That from the hunters' aim had ta'en a hurt,
Did come to languish.'

Shelley doubtless knew Cowper's beautiful lines in **The Task,** Book III (pub-lished in 1785):—

'I was a stricken deer that left the herd,' &c.
He does not elsewhere mention Cowper.

Stanza 34, 1. 1. **His partial moan.** The epithet 'partial' is accounted for by what immediately follows—viz. that Shelley 'in another's fate now wept his own.' He, like Keats, was the object of critical virulence, and he was wont (but on very different grounds) to anticipate an early death. See (on p. 35) the expression in a letter from Shelley—'a writer who, however he may differ,' &c.

1. 2. **Smiled through their tears.** Cp. Homer, **Iliad** vi. 484

11. 4, 5. *As in the accents of an unknown land, He sang new sorrow.* It is not very clear why Shelley should represent that he, as one of the Mountain Shepherds, used a language different (as one might infer) from that of his companions. All those whom he particularizes were his compatriots. Perhaps however Shelley merely means that the language (English) was that of a land unknown to the Greek deity Aphrodite Urania, or to the inhabitants of Rome. The phrase 'new sorrow' occurs in the Elegy by Moschus (p. 69). By the use of this phrase Shelley seems to mean not merely that the death of Keats was a recent and sorrowful event, but more especially that it constituted a new sorrow—one more sorrow—to Shelley himself.

11. 3, 5. I reproduce the punctuation of the Pisan edition, with semicolons after 'his own' and 'sorrow.' It appears to me however that the sense would rather require either a full stop after 'his own,' and a comma after 'sorrow,' or else a comma after 'his own,' and a full stop or colon after 'sorrow.' Yet it is possible that the phrase, 'As in the accents,' &c., forms a separate clause by itself, meaning, 'As *if* in the accents of an unknown land, he sang new sorrow.' The comma which in the Pisan edition follows 'land' makes this probable, the reference being to the Greek form of the *Adonais.*

11. 8, 9. *Made bare his branded and ensanguined brow, Which was like Cain's or Christ's.* Shelley represents his own brow as being branded like Cain's— stamped with the mark of reprobation; and ensanguined like Christ's—bleeding from a crown of thorns. This indicates the extreme repugnance with which he was generally regarded, and in especial perhaps the decree of the Court of Chancery which deprived him of his children by his first marriage—and generally the troubles and sufferings which he had undergone. The close coupling-together, in this line, of the names of Cain and Christ, was not likely to conciliate antagonists; and indeed one may safely surmise that it was done by Shelley more for the rather wanton purpose of exasperating them than with any other object. It might be suggested that the mention of Cain, taken in connexion with the epithets 'branded and ensanguined' in l. 1, points to some genuine touches of remorse for the incidents of the poet's first marriage, and its unhappy end. I do not however think that this was

intended: Shelley seems always to have maintained that he was not in the wrong in that matter. By the naming of Christ in this stanza, and of Cain both in this and in stanza 17, Shelley goes outside the limits of classical allusion. These, if we except the name Albion, are the sole instances, but he has to name some modern poets— Milton, Chatterton, Sidney. In this stanza Urania appears for the last time.

Stanza 35, 1. 1. *What softer voice is hushed over the dead?* The personage here referred to is Leigh Hunt. See p. 46.

1. 6. *Gentlest of the wise.* It is apparent that Shelley entertained a very sincere affection and regard for Leigh Hunt. He dedicated to Hunt the tragedy of *The Cenci,* using the following expressions among others: 'Had I known a person more highly endowed than yourself with all that it becomes a man to possess, I had solicited for this work the ornament of his name. One more gentle, honourable, innocent, and brave; one of more exalted toleration for all who do and think evil, and yet himself more free from evil; one who knows better how to receive and how to confer a benefit, though he must ever confer far more than he can receive; one of simpler and (in the highest sense of the word) of purer life and manners, I never knew: and I had already been fortunate in friendships when your name was added to the list.'

1. 7. *Taught, soothed, loved, honoured, the departed one.* It has sometimes been maintained that Hunt, whatever may have been the personal friendship which he felt for Keats, did not, during the latter's lifetime, champion his literary cause with so much zeal as might have been expected from his professions. This is a point open to a good deal of discussion from both sides. Mr. Buxton Forman, who as Editor of Keats had occasion to investigate the matter attentively, pronounces decidedly in favour of Hunt.

Stanza 36, 1. 1. *Our Adonais has drunk poison.* Founded on those lines of Moschus which appear as a motto to Shelley's Elegy. See also p. 49.

1. 2. *What deaf and viperous murderer.* Deaf, because insensible to the beau-

ty of Keats's verse; and viperous, because poisonous and malignant. The juxtaposition of the two epithets may probably be also partly dependent on that passage in the *Psalms* (lviii. 4, 5) which has become proverbial: 'They are as venomous as the poison of a serpent: even like the deaf adder that stoppeth her ears; which refuseth to hear the voice of the charmer, charm he never so wisely.'

1. 4. *The nameless worm.* A worm, as being one of the lowest forms of life, is constantly used as a term implying contempt; but it may be assumed that Shelley here uses 'worm' in its original sense, that of any crawling creature, more especially of the snake kind. There would thus be no departure from the previous epithet 'viperous.' See the remarks as to 'reptiles,' st. 29.

11. 5, 6. *The magic tone Whose prelude,* &c. Shelley, it will be perceived, here figures Keats as a minstrel striking the lyre, and preparing to sing. He strikes the lyre in a 'magic tone'; the very 'prelude' of this was enough to command silent expectation. This prelude is the poem of *Endymion,* to which the *Quarterly* reviewer alone (according to Shelley) was insensitive, owing to feelings of 'envy, hate, and wrong.' The prelude was only an induction to the 'song,'—which was eventually poured forth in the *Lamia* volume, and especially (as our poet opined) in *Hyperion.* But now Keats's hand is cold in death, and his lyre unstrung. As I have already observed—see p. 36, &c.—Shelley was mistaken in supposing that the *Quarterly Review* had held a monopoly of 'envy, hate, and wrong'—or, as one might now term them, detraction, spite, and unfairness—in reference to Keats.

Stanza 37, 1. 4. *But be thyself, and know thyself to be!* The precise import of this line is not, I think, entirely plain at first sight. I conceive that we should take the line as immediately consequent upon the preceding words—'Live thou, live!' Premising this, one might amplify the idea as follows: 'While Keats is dead, be it thy doom, thou deaf and viperous murderer, to live! But thou shalt live in thine own degraded identity, and shalt thyself be conscious how degraded thou art.' Another suggestion might be that the words 'But be thyself' are equivalent to 'Be but thyself.'

11. 5, 6. ***And ever at thy season be thou free To spill the venom when thy fangs o'erflow.*** This keeps up the image of the 'viperous' murderer—the viper. 'At thy season' can be understood as a reference to the periodical issues of the ***Quarterly Review.*** The word 'o'erflow' is, in the Pisan edition, printed as two words—'o'er flow.'

1. 7. ***Remorse and self-contempt.*** Shelley frequently dwells upon self-contempt as one of the least tolerable of human distresses. Thus in the ***Revolt of Islam*** (canto viii, st. 20):—

'Yes, it is Hate—that shapeless fiendly thing
Of many names, all evil, some divine—
Whom self-contempt arms with a mortal sting,' &c.

And in ***Prometheus Unbound*** (i.):—

'Regard this earth
Made multitudinous with thy slaves, whom thou
Requitest for knee-worship, prayer, and praise,
And toil, and hecatombs of broken hearts,
With fear and self-contempt and barren hope.'

Again (ii. 4):—

'And self-contempt, bitterer to drink than blood.'

Stanza 38, 1. 1. ***Nor let us weep,*** &c. So far as the broad current of sentiment is concerned, this is the turning-point of Shelley's Elegy. Hitherto the tone has been continuously, and through a variety of phases, one of mourning for the fact that Keats, the great poetical genius, is untimely dead. But now the writer pauses, checks himself, and recognizes that mourning is not the only possible feeling, nor indeed the most appropriate one. As his thought expands and his rapture rises, he soon acknowledges that, so far from grieving for Keats who *is* dead, it were far more relevant to grieve for himself who is ***not*** dead. This paean of recantation and aspiration occupies the remainder of the poem.

1. 2. ***These carrion kites.*** A term of disparagement corresponding nearly enough to the 'ravens' and 'vultures' of st. 28.

1. 3. ***He wakes or sleeps with the enduring dead.*** With such of the dead as have done something which survives themselves. It will be observed that the phrase 'he wakes ***or*** sleeps' leaves the question of personal or individual immortality quite open. As to this point see the remarks on p. 55, &c.

1. 4. ***Thou canst not soar where he is sitting now.*** This is again addressed to the 'deaf and viperous murderer,' regarded for the moment as a 'carrion kite.' As kites are eminently high flyers, the phrase here used becomes the more emphatic. This line of Shelley's is obviously adapted from a passage in Milton's ***Paradise Lost,*** where Satan addresses the angels in Eden (Book IV):—

'Ye knew me once, no mate
For you, there sitting where ye durst not soar.'

1. 5. ***The pure spirit shall flow,*** &c. The spirit which once was the vital or mental essence—the soul—of Adonais came from the Eternal Soul, and now that he is dead, is re-absorbed into the Eternal Soul: as such, it is imperishable.

1. 9. ***Whilst thy cold embers choke,*** &c. The spirit of Adonais came as a flame from the '***burning*** fountain' of the Eternal, and has now reverted thither, he being one of the '***enduring*** dead.' But the 'deaf and viperous murderer' must not hope for a like destiny. His spirit, after death, will be merely like 'cold embers,' cumbering the 'hearth of shame.' As a rhetorical antithesis, this serves its purpose well: no doubt Shelley would not have pretended that it is a strictly reasoned antithesis as well, or furnishes a full account of the ***post-mortem*** fate of the ***Quarterly*** reviewer.

Stanza 39, 11. 1, 2. Peace, peace! he is not dead, he doth not sleep—He hath awakened from the dream of lift. *Shelley now proceeds boldly to declare that the state which we call death is to be preferred to that which we call life. Keats is neither dead nor sleeping. He used to be asleep, perturbed and tantalized by the dream which is termed life. Having at last awakened from the dream, he is no longer asleep: and, if life is no more than a dream, neither does the cessation of life deserve to be named death. The transition from one emotion to another in this passage, and also in the preceding stanza, 'Nor let us weep,' &c., resembles the transition towards the close of* Lycidas :—

'Weep no more, woful shepherds, weep no more,
For Lycidas, your sorrow, is not dead,' &c.

The general view has considerable affinity to that which is expounded in a portion of Plato's dialogue *Phaedo,* and which has been thus summarized. 'Death is merely the separation of soul and body. And this is the very consummation at which Philosophy aims: the body hinders thought,—the mind attains to truth by retiring into herself. Through no bodily sense does she perceive justice, beauty, goodness, and other ideas. The philosopher has a lifelong quarrel with bodily desires, and he should welcome the release of his soul.' Cp. Plato, *Gorgias,* p. 492 c:—

The quotation is from the *Polyidus* of Euripides, and there is a very similar passage in his *Phrixus.*

1. 3. *'Tis we who, lost in stormy visions,* &c. We, the so-called living, are in fact merely beset by a series of stormy visions which constitute life; all our efforts are expended upon mere phantoms, and are therefore profitless; our mental conflict is an act of trance, exercised upon mere nothings. The very energetic expression, 'strike with our spirit's knife invulnerable nothings,' is worthy of remark. It will be remembered that, according to Shelley's belief, 'nothing exists but as it is perceived': see p. 57. The view of life expressed with passionate force in this passage of *Adonais* is the same which forms the calm and placid conclusion of *The Sensitive Plant,* a

poem written in 1820 (and indeed nearly the same view is implied in Keats's phrase, 'a thing of beauty is a joy for ever'):—

'But, in this life
Of error, ignorance, and strife,
Where nothing is but all things seem,
And we the shadows of the dream,

It is a modest creed, and yet
Pleasant if one considers it,
To own that death itself must be,
Like all the rest, a mockery.

That garden sweet, that Lady fair,
And all sweet shapes and odours there,
In truth have never passed away:
'Tis we, 'tis ours, are changed; not they.

For love, and beauty, and delight,
There is no death nor change; their might
Exceeds our organs, which endure
No light, being themselves obscure.'

11. 6, 7. *We decay Like corpses in a charnel,* &c. Human life consists of a process of decay. While living, we are consumed by fear and grief; our disappointed hopes swarm in our living persons like worms in our corpses.

Stanza 40, 1. 1. *He has outsoared the shadow of our night.* As human life was in the last stanza represented as a dream, so the state of existence in which it is enacted is here figured as night.

1. 5. *From the contagion of the world's slow stain.* It may be said that 'the world's slow stain'—the lowering influence of the aims and associations of all ordi-

nary human life—is the main subject-matter of Shelley's latest important poem, *The Triumph of Life.*

1. 9. **With sparkless ashes.** See the cognate expression 'thy cold embers,' in st. 38.

Stanza 41, 1. 1. He lives, he wakes—'tis Death is dead, not he. In the preceding three stanzas Adonais is contemplated as being alive, owing to the very fact that his death has awakened him 'from the dream of life'—mundane life. Death has bestowed upon him a vitality superior to that of mundane life. Death therefore has performed an act contrary to his own essence as death, and has practically killed, not Adonais, but himself.

1. 2. **Thou young Dawn.** We here recur to the image in st. 14, 'Morning sought her eastern watch-tower,' &c.

1. 5. **Ye caverns and ye forests,** &c. The poet now adjures the caverns, forests, flowers, fountains, and air, to 'cease to moan.' Of the flowers we had heard in st. 16; but the other features of Nature which are now addressed had not previously been individually mentioned—except, to some extent, by implication, in st. 15, which refers more directly to 'Echo.' The reference to the air had also been, in a certain degree, prepared for in st. 23. The stars are said to smile on the Earth's despair. This does not, I apprehend, indicate any despair of the Earth consequent on the death of Adonais, but a general condition of woe. A reference of a different kind to stars—a figurative reference—appears in st. 29.

Stanza 42, 1. 1. **He is made one with Nature.** This stanza ascribes to Keats the same phase of immortality which belongs to Nature. Having 'awakened from the dream of [mundane] life,' his spirit forms an integral portion of the universe. Those acts of intellect which he performed in the flesh remain with us, as thunder and the song of the nightingale remain with us.

11. 6, 7. **Where'er that Power may move Which has withdrawn his being to**

its own. This corresponds to the expression in st. 38—'The pure spirit shall flow Back to the burning fountain whence it came, A portion of the Eternal.'

1. 8. ***Which wields the world with never wearied love,*** &c. These two lines are about the nearest approach to definite Theism to be found in any writing of Shelley. The conception, which may amount to Theism, is equally consistent with Pantheism. Even in his most anti-theistic poem, ***Queen Mab,*** Shelley said in a note—'The hypothesis of a pervading Spirit, co-eternal with the universe, remains unshaken.'

Stanza 43, 11. 1–3. ***He is a portion of the loveliness Which once he made more lovely. He doth bear His part,*** &c. The conception embodied in this passage may become more clear to the reader if its terms are pondered in connexion with the passage of Shelley's prose extracted on p. 58—'the existence of distinct individual minds,' &c. Keats, while a living man, had made the loveliness of the universe more lovely by expressing in poetry his acute and subtle sense of its beauties—by lavishing on it (as we say) 'the colours of his imagination.' He was then an 'individual mind'—according to the current, but (as Shelley held) inexact terminology. He has now, by death, wholly passed out of the class of individual minds: and he forms a portion of the Universal Mind (the 'One Spirit') which is the animation of the universe.

11. 3, 4. ***While the One Spirit's plastic stress Sweeps through the dull dense world,*** &c. The function ascribed in these lines to the One Spirit is a formative or animating function: the Spirit constitutes the life of 'trees and beasts and men.' This view is strictly within the limits of Pantheism.

Stanza 44, 1. 1. ***The splendours of the firmament of time,*** &c. As there are stars in the firmament of heaven, so are there splendours—luminous intellects—in the firmament of time. The stars, though at times eclipsed, are not extinguished; nor yet the mental luminaries. In stanza 5 Shelley speaks of 'suns' which 'perished,' and poets who sank 'in their refulgent prime.' In the latter part of the poem, following the inspiration of Milton in ***Lycidas,*** he denies the reality of death, though in another sense from Milton's. The great poet may be eclipsed, but does not perish, as did the lost suns. Thus there is some intentional contradiction between the two passages: the later one is a palinode.

11. 5, 6. ***When lofty thought Lifts a young heart,*** &c. The sense of this passage may be paraphrased thus:—When lofty thought lifts a young heart above its mundane environments, and when its earthly doom has to be determined by the conflicting influences of love, which would elevate it, and the meaner cares and interests of life, which would drag it downwards, then the illustrious dead live again in that heart—for its higher emotions are nurtured by their noble thoughts and aspirations,—and they move, like exhalations of light along dark and stormy air. This illustrates the previous proposition, that the splendours of the firmament of time are not extinguished; and, in the most immediate application of the proposition, Keats is not extinguished—he will continue an ennobling influence upon minds struggling towards the light.

Stanza 45, 11. 1, 2. ***The inheritors of unfulfilled renown Rose from their thrones.*** There is a grand abruptness in this phrase, which makes it—as a point of poetical or literary structure—one of the finest things in the Elegy. We are to understand (but Shelley is too great a master to formulate it in words) that Keats, as an 'inheritor of unfulfilled renown'—i. e. a great intellect cut off by death before its maturest fruits could be produced—has now arrived among his compeers: they rise from their thrones to welcome him. In this connexion Shelley chooses to regard Keats as still a living spiritual personality—not simply as 'made one with Nature.' He is one of those 'splendours of the firmament of time' who 'may be eclipsed, but are extinguished not.' With the whole stanza compare Isaiah xiv. 9, 10: 'Hell from beneath is moved for thee, to meet thee at thy coming. . . . It hath raised up from their thrones all the kings of the nations. All they shall speak and say unto thee: "Art thou also become weak as we? art thou become like unto us?"'

11. 3–5. ***Chatterton Rose pale, his solemn agony had not Yet faded from him.*** For precocity and exceptional turn of genius Chatterton was certainly one of the most extraordinary of 'the inheritors of unfulfilled renown'; indeed, ***the*** most extraordinary: he committed suicide by poison in 1770, before completing the eigh-

teenth year of his age. His supposititious modern-antique *Poems of Rowley* may, as actual achievements, have been sometimes overpraised: but at the lowest estimate they have beauties and excellences of the most startling kind. He wrote besides a quantity of verse and prose, of a totally different order. Keats admired Chatterton profoundly, and dedicated *Endymion* to his memory. I cannot find that Shelley, except in *Adonais,* has left any remarks upon Chatterton: but he is said by Captain Medwin to have been, in early youth, very much impressed by his writings.

1. 5. *Sidney, as he fought,* &c. Sir Philip Sidney, author of *The Countess of Pembroke's Arcadia,* the *Apology for Poetry,* and the sonnets named *Astrophel and Stella,* died in his thirty-second year, of a wound received in the battle of Zutphen, 1586. Shelley intimates that Sidney maintained the character of being 'sublimely mild' in fighting, falling (dying), and loving, as well as generally in living. The special references appear to be these. (1) Sidney, observing that the Lord Marshal, the Earl of Leicester, had entered the field of Zutphen without greaves, threw off his own, and thus exposed himself to the cannon-shot which slew him. (2) Being mortally wounded, and receiving a cup of water, he handed it (according to a tradition which is not unquestionable) to a dying soldier. (3) His series of sonnets record his love for Penelope Devereux, sister to the Earl of Essex, who married Lord Rich. She had at one time been promised to Sidney. He wrote the sonnets towards 1581: in 1583 he married another lady, daughter of Sir Francis Walsingham. It has been said that Shelley was wont to make some self-parade in connexion with Sir Philip Sidney, giving it to be understood that he was himself a descendant of the hero—which was not true, although the Sidney blood came into a different line of the family. Of this story I have not found any tangible confirmation.

1. 8. *Lucan, by his death approved.* Lucan, the author of the *Pharsalia,* was condemned under Nero as being an accomplice in the conspiracy of Piso. He was induced to turn informer, and denounced even his own mother: being notwithstanding condemned to death, he caused his veins to be opened, and died magnanimously, aged about twenty-six, A.D. 65. The phrase 'by his death approved' appears to be suggested by Lucan himself, who, in describing the death of Pompey, writes, viii. 620 'Seque probat moriens'; and again, 11. 625–6 'ignorant populi, si non in

morte probaris An scieris adversa pati.' Lucan's views of the merit of such a death, voluntary, or accepted as a necessity, will be found more at length in iv. 474–528. Shelley speaks of Lucan in the ***Defence of Poetry*** as a second-rate poet, as one of the 'mock-birds' 'whose notes were sweet'; but yet with sympathy as of one who, by hard conditions of date and nationality, was forbidden to realize his own genius. He had at an earlier date

band—or, reckoning the lapse of ages as if they were but a day, its 'evening star.' The exceptional brilliancy of the Vesper star is not, I think, implied—though it may be remotely suggested.

Stanza 47, 1. 3. ***Clasp with thy panting soul,*** &c. The significance of this stanza—perhaps a rather obscure one—requires to be estimated as a whole. Shelley summons any person who persists in mourning for Adonais to realize to his own mind what are the true terms of comparison between Adonais and himself. After this, he says in this stanza no more about Adonais, but only about the mourner. He calls upon the mourner to consider (1) the magnitude of the planet earth; then, using the earth as his centre, to consider (2) the whole universe of worlds, and the illimitable void of space beyond all worlds; next he is to consider (3) what he himself is—he is confined within the day and night of our planet, and even within those restricted limits he is but an infinitesimal point. After he shall have realized this to himself, and after the tension of his soul in ranging through the universe and through space shall have kindled hope after hope, wonderment and aspiration after aspiration and wonderment, then indeed will he need to keep his heart light, lest it make him sink at the contemplation of his own nullity.

1. 9. ***And lured thee to the brink.*** This phrase is not definitely accounted for in the preceding exposition. I think Shelley means that the successive hopes kindled in the mourner by the ideas of a boundless universe of space and of spirit will have lured him to the very brink of mundane life—to the borderland between life and death: he will almost have been tempted to have done with life, and to explore the possibilities of death.

Stanza 48, 1. 1. ***Or go to Rome.*** This is still addressed to the mourner, the 'fond wretch' of the preceding stanza. He is here invited to adopt a different test for 'knowing himself and Adonais aright'; namely, he is to visit Rome, and muse over the grave of the youthful poet.

11. 1, 2. ***Which is the sepulchre, Oh not of him, but of our joy.*** Keats is not entombed in Rome: his poor mortal remains are there entombed, and, along with them, the joy which we felt in him as a living and breathing presence.

11. 2, 3. '***Tis nought That ages, empires, and religions,*** &c. Keats, and others such as he, derive no adventitious honour from being buried in Rome, amid the wreck of ages, empires, and religions: rather they confer honour. He is among his peers, the kings of thought who, so far from being dragged down in the ruin of institutions, contended against that ruin, and are alone immortal while all the rest of the past has come to nought. This consideration may be said to qualify, but not to reverse, that which is presented in stanza 7, that Keats 'bought, with price of purest breath, a grave among the eternal'; those eternal ones, buried in Rome, include many of the 'kings of thought.'

Stanza 49, 11. 3, 4. ***And where its wrecks like shattered mountains rise, And flowering weeds,*** &c. These expressions point more especially, but not exclusively, to the Coliseum and the Baths of Caracalla. In Shelley's time (and something alike was the case in 1862, the year when the present writer saw them first) both these vast monuments were in a state wholly different from that which they now, under the hands of learned archaeologists and skilled restorers, present to the eye. Shelley began, probably in 1819, a romantic or ideal tale named ***The Coliseum;*** and, ensconced amid the ruins of the Baths of Caracalla, he composed, in the same year, a large part of ***Prometheus Unbound.*** A few extracts from his letters may here be given appropriately. (To T. L. Peacock, December 22, 1818.) 'The Coliseum is unlike any work of human hands I ever saw before. It is of enormous height and circuit, and the arches, built of massy stones, ore piled on one another, and jut into the blue air, shattered into the forms of overhanging rocks. It has been changed by time into the image of an amphitheatre of rocky hills overgrown by the wild olive, the myrtle, and the figtree, and threaded by little paths which wind among its ruined stairs and immeasurable galleries: the copsewood overshadows you as you wander through its labyrinths.'—(To the same, March 23, 1819.) 'The next most considerable relic of antiquity, considered as a ruin, is the Thermae of Caracalla. These consist of six enormous chambers, above 200 feet in height, and each enclosing a vast space like that of a field. There are in addition a number of towers and labyrinthine recesses, hidden and woven over by the wild growth of weeds and ivy. Never was any desolation so sublime and lovely. . . . At every step the aerial pinnacles of shattered stone group into new combinations of effect, and tower above the lofty yet level walls, as the distant mountains change their aspect to one travelling rapidly along the plain. . . . Around rise other crags and other peaks—all arrayed, and the deformity of their vast desolation softened down, by the undecaying investiture of Nature.'

1. 7. *A slope of green access.* The old Protestant Cemetery. Shelley described it thus in his letter to Mr. Peacock of December 22, 1818: 'The English burying-place is a green slope near the walls, under the pyramidal tomb of Cestius, and is, I think, the most beautiful and solemn cemetery I ever beheld. To see the sun shining on its bright grass, fresh, when we visited it, with the autumnal dews, and hear the whispering of the wind among the leaves of the trees which have overgrown the tomb of Cestius, and the soil which is stirring in the sun-warm earth, and to mark the tombs, mostly of women and young people who were buried there, one might, if one were to die, desire the sleep they seem to sleep. Such is the human mind, and so it peoples with its wishes vacancy and oblivion.'—See also p. 71.

Stanza 50, 1. 3. *One keen pyramid.* The tomb (see last note) of Caius Cestius, a Tribune of the People.

11. 4, 5. *The dust of him who planned This refuge for his memory.* Shelley probably means that this sepulchral pyramid alone preserves to remembrance the name of Cestius: which is true enough, as next to nothing is otherwise known about him.

1. 8. *Have pitched in heaven's smile their camp of death.* The practice which

Shelley follows in this line of making 'heaven' a dissyllable is very frequent with him. So also with 'even, higher,' and other such words.

Stanza 51, 11. 3, 4. ***If the seal is set Here on one fountain of a mourning mind.*** Shelley certainly alludes to himself in this line. His beloved son William, who died in June 1819, in the fourth year of his age, was buried in this cemetery: the precise spot is not now known.

11. 5–7. ***Too surely shalt thou find Thine own well full, if thou returnest home, Of tears and gall. From the world's bitter wind,*** &c. The apposition between the word 'well' and the preceding word 'fountain' will be observed. The person whom Shelley addresses would, on returning home from the cemetery, find more than ample cause, of one sort or another, for distress and discomposure. Hence follows the conclusion that he would do well to 'seek shelter in the shadow of the tomb': he should prefer the condition of death to that of life. And so we reach in stanza 51 the same result which, in stanza 47, was deduced from a different range of considerations.

Stanza 52, 1. 1. ***The One remains, the many change and pass.*** The language and thought of this stanza are Platonic. It was a problem of early philosophy to find the One in the many. Thus Parmenides and the Eleatics taught that the One only is, while the many, i. e. the phenomena of the material universe, are not. And so the Platonic Socrates is made to say (***Phaedrus*** 266, Jowett's Translation): 'If I find any man who is able to see "a One and Many" in nature, him I follow, and walk in his footsteps, as if he were a god." Line 2 recalls the famous image of the cave in Plato's ***Republic*** : men are chained in a cave, and can only see the shadows cast upon a wall by figures passing between it and a light at which they cannot bear to look directly. The beautiful image of the many colours and the one bright radiance which they stain may have been suggested by Plato's scheme of colours given in the ***Timaeus,*** but, as here presented, it is Shelley's own.

11. 3–5. ***Lift, like a dome of many-coloured glass, Stains the white radiance***

of eternity, Until Death tramples it to fragments. Two different views have been taken as to the essential meaning of these lines. My own view is that, while eternity is here figured as white light—light in its quintessence—life, mundane life, is figured as a dome of glass (or, as one might say, an immense glass bubble), which becomes many-coloured by its prismatic refraction of the white light. Death ultimately tramples the glass dome into fragments: each individual life is shattered, and integral life, made up of many individual lives, is shattered. This I regard as a metaphorical symbol as daring, and with as deep and spacious a meaning, as any that has been employed by any poet. A consummate image, vast in purport, and terse in form. A second view, which appears to me sadly to reduce the importance of the symbol, is that the dome of glass is 'many-coloured' in the literal sense—stained glass of various hues. This is certainly not inconsistent with the diction of the passage, but I demur to accepting it as correct.

ll. 5, 6. *Die, If thou wouldst be with that which thou dost seek.* This phrase is addressed by the poet to anybody, and more especially to himself. As in stanza 38—'the pure spirit shall flow Back to the burning fountain whence it came, A portion of the Eternal.'

ll. 7–9. *Rome's azure sky, Flowers, ruins, statues, music, words, are weak The glory they transfuse with fitting truth to speak.* I follow here the punctuation of the Pisan edition—with a comma after 'words,' as well as after 'sky, flowers,' &c. According to this punctuation, the words of Rome, as well as her sky and other beautiful endowments, are too weak to declare at full the glory which they impart; and the inference from this rather abruptly introduced recurrence to Rome is (I suppose), that the spiritual glory faintly adumbrated by Rome can only be realized in that realm of eternity to which death gives access. Taken in this sense, the 'words' of Rome appear to mean 'the beautiful language spoken in Rome'—the Roman or Latin language, as modified into modern Italian. The pronunciation of Italian in Rome is counted peculiarly pure and rich: hence the Italian adage, 'lingua toscana in bocca romana'—Tuscan tongue in Roman mouth. At first sight, it would seem far more natural to punctuate thus: 'Rome's azure sky, Flowers, ruins, statues, music,—words are weak The glory,' &c. The sense would then be—Words are too weak to declare at full the glory inherent in the sky, flowers, &c. of Rome. Yet, although this seems a more straightforward arrangement for the words of the sentence, as such, it is not clear that such a comment on the beauties of Rome would have any great relevancy in its immediate context.

Stanza 53, 1. 2. ***Thy hopes are gone before,*** &c. This stanza contains some very pointed references to the state of Shelley's feelings at the time when he was writing ***Adonais;*** pointed, but not so clearly defined as to make his actual meaning transparent. We are told that his hopes are gone before (i. e. have vanished before the close of his life has come), and have departed from all things here. This may partly refer to the deaths of William Shelley and of Keats; but I think the purport of the phrase extends further, and implies that Shelley's hopes generally—those animating conceptions which had inspired him in early youth, and had buoyed him up through many adversities—are now waning in disappointment. This is confirmed by the ensuing statement—that 'A light is past from the revolving year [a phrase repeated from stanza 18], And man and woman.' Next we are told that 'what still is dear Attracts to crush, repels to make thee [me] wither.' The ***persons*** who were more particularly dear to Shelley at this time must have been (not to mention the two children Percy Florence Shelley and Allegra Clairmont) his wife, Miss Clairmont, Emilia Viviani, and Lieutenant and Mrs. Williams: Byron, Leigh Hunt, and Godwin can hardly be in question. No doubt Shelley's acute feelings and mobile sympathies involved him in some considerable agitations, from time to time, with all the four ladies here named: but the strong expressions which he uses as to attracting and repelling, crushing and withering, seem hardly likely to have been employed by him in this personal sense in a published book. Perhaps therefore we shall be safest in supposing that he alludes, not to ***persons*** who are dear, but to circumstances and conditions of a more general kind—such as are involved in his self-portraiture, stanzas 31–34.

1. 8. '***Tis Adonais calls! Oh hasten thither!*** 'Thither' may mean 'to Adonais': a laxity of expression. Or it may apply, with vagueness of reference, to the region to which Adonais has now migrated.

Stanza 54, 1. 1. ***That light whose smile kindles the universe,*** &c. This is again the 'One Spirit' of stanza 43. And see, in stanza 42, the cognate expression, 'kindles it above.'

11. 3, 4. ***That benediction which the eclipsing curse Of birth can quench not.*** The curse of birth is, I think, simply the calamitous condition of mundane life— so often referred to in this Elegy as a condition of abjection and unhappiness. The curse of birth can eclipse the benediction of Universal Mind, but cannot quench it: in other words, the human mind, in its passage from the birth to the death of the body, is still an integral portion of the Universal Mind.

1. 7. ***Each are mirrors.*** This is of course a grammatical irregularity—the verb should be 'is.' It is not the only instance of the same kind in Shelley's poetry.

1. 9. ***Consuming the last clouds of cold mortality.*** This does not imply that Shelley is shortly about to die. 'Cold mortality' is that condition in which the human mind, a portion of the Universal Mind, is united to a mortal body: and the general sense is that the Universal Mind at this moment beams with such effulgence upon Shelley that his mind responds to it as if the mortal body no longer interposed any impediment.

Stanza 55, 1. 1. ***The breath whose might I have invoked in song.*** The breath or afflatus of the Universal Mind. It has been 'invoked in song' throughout the whole later section of this Elegy, from stanza 38 onwards.

1. 2. ***My spirit's bark is driven,*** &c. As was observed with reference to the preceding stanza, line 9, this phrase does not forecast the author's death: it only re-emphasizes the abnormal illumination of his mind by the Universal Mind—as if his spirit (like that of Keats) had flowed 'Back to the burning fountain whence it came, A portion of the Eternal' (stanza 38). Nevertheless, it is very remarkable that this image of 'the spirit's ***bark,*** ' beaconed by 'the soul of Adonais,' should have been written so soon before Shelley's death by drowning, which occurred on July 8, 1822,—but little more than a year after he had completed this Elegy. Besides this

passage, there are in Shelley's writings, both verse and prose, several other passages noticeable on the same account—relating to drowning, and sometimes with a strong personal application; and in various instances he was in imminent danger of this mode of death before the end came.

11. 3, 4. *Far from the shore, far from the trembling throng Whose sails were never to the tempest given.* In saying that his spirit's bark is driven far from the shore, Shelley apparently means that his mind, in speculation and aspiration, ranges far beyond those mundane and material interests with which the mass of men are ordinarily concerned. 'The trembling throng' is, I think, a throng of men: though it might be a throng of barks, contrasted with 'my spirit's bark.' Their sails 'were never to the tempest given,' in the sense that they never set forth on a bold ideal or spiritual adventure, abandoning themselves to the stress and sway of a spiritual storm.

1. 5. *The massy earth,* &c. As the poet launches forth on his voyage upon the ocean of mind, the earth behind him seems to gape, and the sky above him to open: his course however is still held on in darkness—the arcanum is hardly or not at all revealed.

1. 7. *Whilst, burning through the inmost veil,* &c. A star pilots his course: it is the soul of Adonais, which, being still 'a portion of the Eternal' (st. 38), is in 'the abode where the Eternal are,' and testifies to the eternity of mind. In this passage, and in others towards the conclusion of the poem, we find the nearest approach which Shelley can furnish to an answer to that question which he asked in stanza 20—'Shall that alone which knows Be as a sword consumed before the sheath By sightless lightning?'

Cancelled Passages of Adonais, Preface. These are taken from Dr. Garnett's *Relics of Shelley,* published in 1862. He says: 'Among Shelley's MSS. is a fair copy of the *Defence of Poetry,* apparently damaged by sea-water, and illegible in many places. Being prepared for the printer, it is written on one side of the paper only: on the blank pages, but frequently undecipherable for the reason just indicated, are many passages intended for, but eventually omitted from, the preface to **Adonais.**'

11. 7–11. *I have employed my poetical compositions and publications simply as the instruments of that sympathy between myself and others which the ardent and unbounded love I cherished for my kind incited me to acquire.* This is an important indication of the spirit in which Shelley wrote, and consequently of that in which his reader should construe his writings. He poured out his full heart, craving for 'sympathy.' Loving mankind, he wished to find some love in response.

1. 21. *Domestic conspiracy and legal oppression,* &c. The direct reference here is to the action taken by Shelley's father-in-law and sister-in-law, Mr. and Miss Westbrook, which resulted in the decree of Lord Chancellor Eldon whereby Shelley was deprived of the custody of the two children of his first marriage. See p. 12.

11. 28–30. *As a bankrupt thief turns thief-taker in despair, so an unsuccessful author turns critic.* Various writers have said something of this kind. I am not sure how far back the sentiment can be traced; but I presume that Shelley was not the first. Some readers will remember a passage in the dedication to his *Peter Bell the Third* (1819), which forestalled Macaulay's famous phrase about the 'New Zealander on the ruins of London Bridge.' Shelley wrote: 'In the firm expectation that, when London shall be an habitation of bitterns; . . . when the piers of Waterloo Bridge shall become the nuclei of islets of reeds and osiers, and cast the jagged shadows of their broken arches on the solitary stream; some Transatlantic commentator will be weighing, in the scales of some new and now unimagined system of criticism, the respective merits of the Bells and the Fudges, and their historians, I remain,' &c.

11. 39, 40. *The offence of this poor victim seems to have consisted solely in his intimacy with Leigh Hunt,* &c. See the remarks on p. 46. There can be no doubt that Shelley was substantially correct in this opinion. Not only the **Quarterly Re-**

view, of which he knew, but also ***Blackwood's Magazine,*** which did not come under his notice, abused Keats because he was personally acquainted with Hunt, and was, in one degree or another, a member of the literary coterie in which Hunt held a foremost place. And Hunt was in bad odour with these reviews because he was a hostile politician, still more than because of any actual or assumed defects in his performances as an ordinary man of letters.

1. 40. ***Mr. Hazlitt.*** William Hazlitt was (it need scarcely be said) a miscellaneous writer of much influence in these years, in politics an advanced Liberal. A selection of his writings was issued by Mr. Alexander Ireland in 1889, and of late years a large amount of attention and eulogium has once more been bestowed upon Hazlitt. Keats admired Hazlitt much more than Hunt.

1. 46. ***I wrote to him, suggesting the propriety,*** &c. See pp. 14, 15.

Cancelled Passages of Adonais (the poem). These passages also were in the first instance published in the ***Shelley Relics*** of Dr. Garnett. They come, not from the same MS. which contains the prefatory fragments, but from some of Shelley's notebooks.

Stanza 1, 1. 1. ***And the green paradise,*** &c. The green paradise is the 'Emerald Isle'—Ireland. This stanza refers to Thomas Moore, and would have followed on after st. 30 in the body of the poem.

Stanza 2, 11. 1, 2. ***And ever as he went he swept a lyre Of unaccustomed shape.*** 'He' has always hitherto, I think, been understood as the 'one frail form' of st. 31—i. e. Shelley himself. The lyre might be of unaccustomed shape for the purpose of indicating that Shelley's poetry differs very essentially, in tone and treatment, from that of other writers. But I incline to think that Shelley, in this stanza, refers not to himself but to Moore. Moore was termed a 'lyrist,' and here we are told about his lyre. The latter would naturally be the Irish harp, and therefore 'of unaccustomed shape': the concluding reference to 'ever-during green' might again glance at the 'Emerald Isle.' As to Shelley, he was stated in st. 33 to be carrying 'a light spear': if he was constantly sweeping a lyre as well, he must have had his hands rather full.

1. 3. ***Now like the . . . of impetuous fire,*** &c. Shelley compares the strains of the lyre—the spirit of the poetry—to two things: (1) to a conflagration in a forest; and (2) to the rustling of wind among the trees. The former image may be understood to apply principally to the revolutionary audacity and fervour of the ideas expressed; the latter, to those qualities of imagination, fantasy, beauty, and melody, which characterize the verse. Of course all this would be more genuinely appropriate to Shelley himself than to Moore: still it would admit of *some* application to Moore, of whom our poet spoke highly more than once elsewhere. The image of a forest on fire is more fully expressed in a passage from the ***Lines written among the Euganean Hills,*** composed by him in 1818:—

'Now new fires from antique light
Spring beneath the wide world's might,—
But their spark lies dead in thee [i. e. in Padua],
Trampled out by Tyranny.
As the Norway woodman quells,
In the depths of piny dells,
One light flame among the brakes,
While the boundless forest shakes,
And its mighty trunks are torn,
By the fire thus lowly born;—
The spark beneath his feet is dead;
He starts to see the flames it fed
Howling through the darkened sky
With a myriad tongues victoriously,
And sinks down in fear;—so thou,
O Tyranny! beholdest now
Light around thee, and thou hearest
The loud flames ascend, and fearest.
Grovel on the earth! ay, hide
In the dust thy purple pride!'

Stanza 3, 1. 1. ***And then came one of sweet and earnest looks.*** It is sufficiently clear that this stanza, and also the fragmentary beginning of stanza 4, refer to Leigh Hunt—who, in the body of the Elegy, is introduced in st. 35. The reader will ob-serve, on looking back to that stanza, that the present one could not be ***added on*** to the description of Hunt: it is an alternative form, ultimately rejected. Its tone is ultra-sentimental, and perhaps on that account it was condemned. The simile at the close of the present stanza is ambitious, but by no means felicitous.

Stanza 4, 11. 1, 2. ***His song, though very sweet, was low and faint, A simple strain.*** It may be doubted whether this description of Hunt's poetry, had it been published in ***Adonais,*** would have been wholly pleasing to Hunt. Neither does it define, with any exceptional aptness, the particular calibre of that poetry.

Stanza 5, 11. 1, 2. ***A mighty Phantasm, half concealed In darkness of his own exceeding light.*** It seems to have been generally assumed that Shelley, in this stan-za, describes one more of the 'Mountain Shepherds' (see st. 30)—viz. Coleridge. No doubt, if ***any*** poet or person is here indicated, it must be Coleridge: and the affirma-tive assumption is so far confirmed by the fact that in another poem—the ***Letter to Maria Gisborne,*** 1820—Shelley spoke of Coleridge in terms partly similar to these:—

'You will see Coleridge; he who sits obscure
In the exceeding lustre and the pure
Intense irradiation of a mind
Which, with its own internal lightning blind,
Flags wearily through darkness and despair—
A cloud-encircled meteor of the air,
A hooded eagle among blinking owls.'

But the first question is—Does this cancelled stanza relate to a Mountain Shep-herd at all? To speak of a Mountain Shepherd as a 'mighty Phantasm,' having an 'awful presence unrevealed,' seems to be taking a considerable liberty with language. To me it appears more likely that the stanza relates to some abstract impersonation—perhaps Death, or else Eternity. It is true that Death figures elsewhere in *Adonais* (stanzas 7, 8, 25) under an aspect with which the present phrases are hardly consistent: but, in the case of a cancelled stanza, that counts for very little. In *Prometheus Unbound* (Act ii, sc. 4) Eternity, symbolized in Demogorgon, is described in terms not wholly unlike those which we are now debating:—

'I see a mighty Darkness
Filling the seat of power, and rays of gloom
Dart round, as light from the meridian sun,
Ungazed upon and shapeless. Neither limb,
Nor form, nor outline; yet we feel it is
A living Spirit.'

As to the phrase in the cancelled stanza, 'In darkness of his own exceeding light,' it need hardly be observed that this is modified from the expression in *Paradise Lost* (Book III):—

'Dark with excessive bright thy skirts appear.'

1. 5. ***Thunder-smoke, whose skirts were chrysolite.*** Technically, chrysolite is synonymous with the precious stone peridot, or olivine—its tint is a yellowish green. But probably Shelley thought only of the primary meaning of the word chrysolite, 'golden-stone,' and his phrase as a whole comes to much the same thing as 'a cloud with a golden lining.'

Stanza 6, 1. 1. ***And like a sudden meteor.*** We here have a fragmentary simile which may—or equally well may not—follow on as connected with st. 5. See on p. 155, for whatever it may be worth in illustration, the line relating to Coleridge:—

'A cloud-encircled meteor of the air.'

1. 5. ***Pavilioned in its tent of light.*** Shelley was fond of the word Pavilion, whether as substantive or as verb. See st. 50: 'Pavilioning the dust of him,' &c.

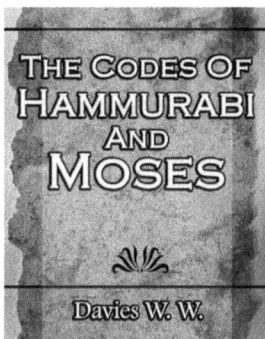

The Codes Of Hammurabi And Moses
W. W. Davies

QTY

The discovery of the Hammurabi Code is one of the greatest achievements of archaeology, and is of paramount interest, not only to the student of the Bible, but also to all those interested in ancient history...

Religion   ISBN: *1-59462-338-4*   Pages:132
MSRP $12.95

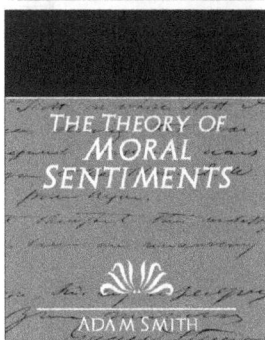

The Theory of Moral Sentiments
Adam Smith

QTY

This work from 1749. contains original theories of conscience amd moral judgment and it is the foundation for systemof morals.

Philosophy   ISBN: *1-59462-777-0*   Pages:536
MSRP $19.95

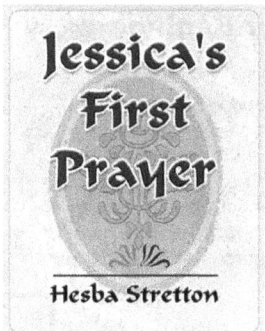

Jessica's First Prayer
Hesba Stretton

QTY

In a screened and secluded corner of one of the many railway-bridges which span the streets of London there could be seen a few years ago, from five o'clock every morning until half past eight, a tidily set-out coffee-stall, consisting of a trestle and board, upon which stood two large tin cans, with a small fire of charcoal burning under each so as to keep the coffee boiling during the early hours of the morning when the work-people were thronging into the city on their way to their daily toil...

Childrens   ISBN: *1-59462-373-2*   Pages:84
MSRP $9.95

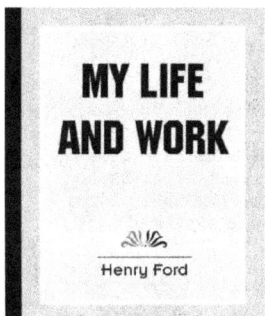

My Life and Work
Henry Ford

QTY

Henry Ford revolutionized the world with his implementation of mass production for the Model T automobile. Gain valuable business insight into his life and work with his own auto-biography... "We have only started on our development of our country we have not as yet, with all our talk of wonderful progress, done more than scratch the surface. The progress has been wonderful enough but..."

Biographies/   ISBN: *1-59462-198-5*   Pages:300
MSRP $21.95

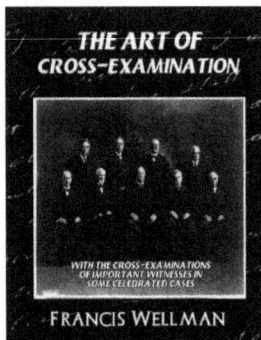

The Art of Cross-Examination
Francis Wellman

QTY

I presume it is the experience of every author, after his first book is published upon an important subject, to be almost overwhelmed with a wealth of ideas and illustrations which could readily have been included in his book, and which to his own mind, at least, seem to make a second edition inevitable. Such certainly was the case with me; and when the first edition had reached its sixth impression in five months, I rejoiced to learn that it seemed to my publishers that the book had met with a sufficiently favorable reception to justify a second and considerably enlarged edition. ..

Pages:412

Reference   **ISBN:** *1-59462-647-2*   *MSRP $19.95*

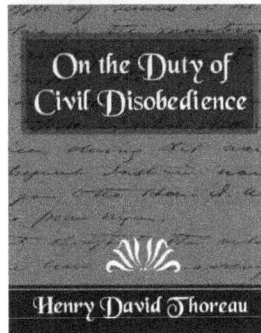

On the Duty of Civil Disobedience
Henry David Thoreau

QTY

Thoreau wrote his famous essay, On the Duty of Civil Disobedience, as a protest against an unjust but popular war and the immoral but popular institution of slave-owning. He did more than write—he declined to pay his taxes, and was hauled off to gaol in consequence. Who can say how much this refusal of his hastened the end of the war and of slavery ?

Law   **ISBN:** *1-59462-747-9*   **Pages:48**

MSRP $7.45

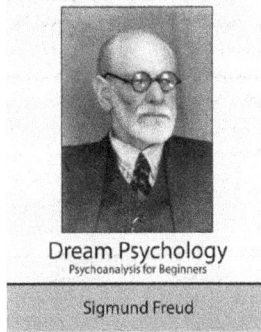

Dream Psychology Psychoanalysis for Beginners
Sigmund Freud

QTY

Sigmund Freud, born Sigismund Schlomo Freud (May 6, 1856 - September 23, 1939), was a Jewish-Austrian neurologist and psychiatrist who co-founded the psychoanalytic school of psychology. Freud is best known for his theories of the unconscious mind, especially involving the mechanism of repression; his redefinition of sexual desire as mobile and directed towards a wide variety of objects; and his therapeutic techniques, especially his understanding of transference in the therapeutic relationship and the presumed value of dreams as sources of insight into unconscious desires.

Pages:196

Psychology   **ISBN:** *1-59462-905-6*   *MSRP $15.45*

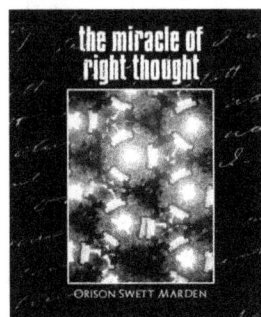

The Miracle of Right Thought
Orison Swett Marden

QTY

Believe with all of your heart that you will do what you were made to do. When the mind has once formed the habit of holding cheerful, happy, prosperous pictures, it will not be easy to form the opposite habit. It does not matter how improbable or how far away this realization may see, or how dark the prospects may be, if we visualize them as best we can, as vividly as possible, hold tenaciously to them and vigorously struggle to attain them, they will gradually become actualized, realized in the life. But a desire, a longing without endeavor, a yearning abandoned or held indifferently will vanish without realization.

Pages:360

Self Help   **ISBN:** *1-59462-644-8*   *MSRP $25.45*

The Rosicrucian Cosmo-Conception Mystic Christianity by *Max Heindel*   ISBN: *1-59462-188-8*   **$38.95**
The Rosicrucian Cosmo-conception is not dogmatic, neither does it appeal to any other authority than the reason of the student. It is: not controversial, but is: sent forth in the, hope that it may help to clear...   New Age/Religion Pages 646

Abandonment To Divine Providence by *Jean-Pierre de Caussade*   ISBN: *1-59462-228-0*   **$25.95**
"The Rev. Jean Pierre de Caussade was one of the most remarkable spiritual writers of the Society of Jesus in France in the 18th Century. His death took place at Toulouse in 1751. His works have gone through many editions and have been republished...   Inspirational/Religion Pages 400

Mental Chemistry by *Charles Haanel*   ISBN: *1-59462-192-6*   **$23.95**
Mental Chemistry allows the change of material conditions by combining and appropriately utilizing the power of the mind. Much like applied chemistry creates something new and unique out of careful combinations of chemicals the mastery of mental chemistry...   New Age Pages 354

The Letters of Robert Browning and Elizabeth Barret Barrett 1845-1846 vol II   ISBN: *1-59462-193-4*   **$35.95**
by *Robert Browning and Elizabeth Barrett*   Biographies Pages 596

Gleanings In Genesis (volume I) by *Arthur W. Pink*   ISBN: *1-59462-130-6*   **$27.45**
Appropriately has Genesis been termed "the seed plot of the Bible" for in it we have, in germ form, almost all of the great doctrines which are afterwards fully developed in the books of Scripture which follow...   Religion/Inspirational Pages 420

The Master Key by *L. W. de Laurence*   ISBN: *1-59462-001-6*   **$30.95**
In no branch of human knowledge has there been a more lively increase of the spirit of research during the past few years than in the study of Psychology, Concentration and Mental Discipline. The requests for authentic lessons in Thought Control, Mental Discipline and...   New Age/Business Pages 422

The Lesser Key Of Solomon Goetia by *L. W. de Laurence*   ISBN: *1-59462-092-X*   **$9.95**
This translation of the first book of the "Lernegton" which is now for the first time made accessible to students of Talismanic Magic was done, after careful collation and edition, from numerous Ancient Manuscripts in Hebrew, Latin, and French...   New Age/Occult Pages 92

Rubaiyat Of Omar Khayyam by *Edward Fitzgerald*   ISBN:*1-59462-332-5*   **$13.95**
Edward Fitzgerald, whom the world has already learned, in spite of his own efforts to remain within the shadow of anonymity, to look upon as one of the rarest poets of the century, was born at Bredfield, in Suffolk, on the 31st of March, 1809. He was the third son of John Purcell...   Music Pages 172

Ancient Law by *Henry Maine*   ISBN: *1-59462-128-4*   **$29.95**
The chief object of the following pages is to indicate some of the earliest ideas of mankind, as they are reflected in Ancient Law, and to point out the relation of those ideas to modern thought.   Religion/History Pages 452

Far-Away Stories by *William J. Locke*   ISBN: *1-59462-129-2*   **$19.45**
"Good wine needs no bush, but a collection of mixed vintages does. And this book is just such a collection. Some of the stories I do not want to remain buried for ever in the museum files of dead magazine-numbers an author's not unpardonable vanity..."   Fiction Pages 272

Life of David Crockett by *David Crockett*   ISBN: *1-59462-250-7*   **$27.45**
"Colonel David Crockett was one of the most remarkable men of the times in which he lived. Born in humble life, but gifted with a strong will, an indomitable courage, and unremitting perseverance...   Biographies/New Age Pages 424

Lip-Reading by *Edward Nitchie*   ISBN: *1-59462-206-X*   **$25.95**
Edward B. Nitchie, founder of the New York School for the Hard of Hearing, now the Nitchie School of Lip-Reading, Inc, wrote "LIP-READING Principles and Practice". The development and perfecting of this meritorious work on lip-reading was an undertaking...   How-to Pages 400

A Handbook of Suggestive Therapeutics, Applied Hypnotism, Psychic Science   ISBN: *1-59462-214-0*   **$24.95**
by *Henry Munro*   Health/New Age/Health/Self-help Pages 376

A Doll's House: and Two Other Plays by *Henrik Ibsen*   ISBN: *1-59462-112-8*   **$19.95**
Henrik Ibsen created this classic when in revolutionary 1848 Rome. Introducing some striking concepts in playwriting for the realist genre, this play has been studied the world over.   Fiction/Classics/Plays 308

The Light of Asia by *sir Edwin Arnold*   ISBN: *1-59462-204-3*   **$13.95**
In this poetic masterpiece, Edwin Arnold describes the life and teachings of Buddha. The man who was to become known as Buddha to the world was born as Prince Gautama of India but he rejected the worldly riches and abandoned the reigns of power when...   Religion/History/Biographies Pages 170

The Complete Works of Guy de Maupassant by *Guy de Maupassant*   ISBN: *1-59462-157-8*   **$16.95**
"For days and days, nights and nights, I had dreamed of that first kiss which was to consecrate our engagement, and I knew not on what spot I should put my lips..."   Fiction/Classics Pages 240

The Art of Cross-Examination by *Francis L. Wellman*   ISBN: *1-59462-309-0*   **$26.95**
Written by a renowned trial lawyer, Wellman imparts his experience and uses case studies to explain how to use psychology to extract desired information through questioning.   How-to/Science/Reference Pages 408

Answered or Unanswered? by *Louisa Vaughan*   ISBN: *1-59462-248-5*   **$10.95**
Miracles of Faith in China   Religion Pages 112

The Edinburgh Lectures on Mental Science (1909) by *Thomas*   ISBN: *1-59462-008-3*   **$11.95**
This book contains the substance of a course of lectures recently given by the writer in the Queen Street Hall, Edinburgh. Its purpose is to indicate the Natural Principles governing the relation between Mental Action and Material Conditions...   New Age/Psychology Pages 148

Ayesha by *H. Rider Haggard*   ISBN: *1-59462-301-5*   **$24.95**
Verily and indeed it is the unexpected that happens! Probably if there was one person upon the earth from whom the Editor of this, and of a certain previous history, did not expect to hear again...   Classics Pages 380

Ayala's Angel by *Anthony Trollope*   ISBN: *1-59462-352-X*   **$29.95**
The two girls were both pretty, but Lucy who was twenty-one who supposed to be simple and comparatively unattractive, whereas Ayala was credited, as her Bombwhat romantic name might show, with poetic charm and a taste for romance. Ayala when her father died was nineteen...   Fiction Pages 484

The American Commonwealth by *James Bryce*   ISBN: *1-59462-286-8*   **$34.45**
An interpretation of American democratic political theory. It examines political mechanics and society from the perspective of Scotsman James Bryce   Politics Pages 572

Stories of the Pilgrims by *Margaret P. Pumphrey*   ISBN: *1-59462-116-0*   **$17.95**
This book explores pilgrims religious oppression in England as well as their escape to Holland and eventual crossing to America on the Mayflower, and their early days in New England...   History Pages 268

QTY

The Fasting Cure *by Sinclair Upton*
ISBN: *1-59462-222-1* **$13.95**

In the Cosmopolitan Magazine for May, 1910, and in the Contemporary Review (London) for April, 1910, I published an article dealing with my experiences in fasting. I have written a great many magazine articles, but never one which attracted so much attention... New Age/Self Help/Health Pages 164

Hebrew Astrology *by Sepharial*
ISBN: *1-59462-308-2* **$13.45**

In these days of advanced thinking it is a matter of common observation that we have left many of the old landmarks behind and that we are now pressing forward to greater heights and to a wider horizon than that which represented the mind-content of our progenitors... Astrology Pages 144

Thought Vibration or The Law of Attraction in the Thought World
ISBN: *1-59462-127-6* **$12.95**

by William Walker Atkinson
Psychology/Religion Pages 144

Optimism *by Helen Keller*
ISBN: *1-59462-108-X* **$15.95**

Helen Keller was blind, deaf, and mute since 19 months old, yet famously learned how to overcome these handicaps, and spread her lectures promoting optimism. An inspiring read for everyone... Biographies/Inspirational Pages 84

Sara Crewe *by Frances Burnett*
ISBN: *1-59462-360-0* **$9.45**

In the first place, Miss Minchin lived in London. Her home was a large, dull, tall one, in a large, dull square, where all the houses were alike, and all the sparrows were alike, and where all the door-knockers made the same heavy sound... Childrens/Classic Pages 88

The Autobiography of Benjamin Franklin *by Benjamin Franklin*
ISBN: *1-59462-135-7* **$24.95**

The Autobiography of Benjamin Franklin has probably been more extensively read than any other American historical work, and no other book of its kind has had such ups and downs of fortune. Franklin lived for many years in England, where he was agent... Biographies/History Pages 332

Name	
Email	
Telephone	
Address	
City, State ZIP	

☐ **Credit Card**   ☐ **Check / Money Order**

Credit Card Number	
Expiration Date	
Signature	

Please Mail to: Book Jungle
PO Box 2226
Champaign, IL 61825
or Fax to: 630-214-0564

ORDERING INFORMATION

web*: www.bookjungle.com*
email*: sales@bookjungle.com*
fax*: 630-214-0564*
mail*: Book Jungle PO Box 2226 Champaign, IL 61825*
or PayPal *to sales@bookjungle.com*

Please contact us for bulk discounts

DIRECT-ORDER TERMS

**20% Discount if You Order
Two or More Books**
Free Domestic Shipping!
Accepted: Master Card, Visa,
Discover, American Express

www.ingramcontent.com/pod-product-compliance
Lightning Source LLC
Chambersburg PA
CBHW080531090426
42733CB00015B/2554